It suggests that non-material energy forces produced matter, life, and spirit. Physicists already know that energy produced matter.

If energy forces also produced life, then cancer may be caused by malfunctions of energy forces rather than malfunctions of chemical particles. This too can be tested here and now. If energy forces produced spirit, then man's most precious possession can be removed from metaphysics and brought into classrooms and laboratories for study and observation.

Faith is defined as a natural force of energy regenerating the spirit and it possesses the same potential for good or evil as all other energy forces.

Revelation is defined as a natural instrument for the acquisition of all knowledge.

Life is defined as the process by which the universe reveals itself to all living creatures.

Consciousness is identified as the measure of fitness in evolution and is the indicator of evolutionary progress or degeneration. The book states that no product created by man has meaning or purpose except in relation to man, its creator. Man himself can find no meaning and purpose in life except in relation to his Creator.

It is likely that a few of these propositions may be in error. It is certain that further research will result in vast improvements. This is the road of progress in knowledge. But the ideas presented in this book can provoke debate that may help restore youthful exuberance to aged and tired concepts.

About the Author

Born in Galicia, Poland, Alexander Wilf came to the United States at the age of four. With his four brothers, he became a successful businessman in Philadelphia. Mr. Wilf has served as Executive Director and Vice President of the Committee for a Jewish Army, the Emergency Committee to Save the Jewish People of Europe, and the American League for a Free Palestine. He has had a lifelong interest in philosophy and science. He is the co-author, with Samuel Merlin, of *The Ascent of Man*.

Origin and Destiny of the Moral Species

Origin and Destiny of the Moral Species

Alexander Wilf

South Brunswick · New York: A.S. Barnes and Co.
London: Thomas Yoseloff Ltd

© 1969 by A. S. Barnes and Co., Inc.
Library of Congress Catalogue Card Number: 68-27261

A. S. Barnes and Co., Inc.
Cranbury, New Jersey 08512

Thomas Yoseloff Ltd
108 New Bond Street
London W1Y OQX, England

SBN 498-06855-2
Printed in the United States of America

This book is dedicated to the memory of Morton A. Rosenfeld. We had discussed many things during the fourteen long months of his struggle for life. Many of the insights in this book were formulated as a result of these discussions.

Preface

This book is the result of a twenty-year search for the origin and destiny of man. This subject was not approached through metaphysics or theology. It could be described as philosophy in the sense that every science must first establish a philosophy of the subject under investigation. It is not an abstract philosophy. The declared intention is to present it for further scientific research with the goal of entering the arena of knowledge.

My approach is different because I addressed myself not only to scientific language and scientific sources for answers, but also to language and sources which have been the exclusive domain of theology. I am not attempting to harmonize science with religion. Each has its own rules which do not permit compromise. We chose to pursue the matter through obedience to the rules of knowledge. However, there is no rule which requires one to begin with Darwin's origin and evolution through his concept of random mutations guided by natural selection. One may also begin with

"In the beginning God created the heaven and earth."

We have the right to address ourselves to any source of information provided we proceed under the rules of knowledge and submit our findings in the framework of scientific discipline. For example, the political sciences did not hesitate to utilize biblical sources in developing constitutional forms of government for the free world. They arrived at politically scientific conclusions without becoming involved in dogmas and beliefs.

In my thesis I have addressed myself to the Creator rather than to God. I did this because I am asking questions concerning origin or creation and subsequent evolution, not searching for the name, identity, nature, or characteristics of God. I also asked the questions of Darwin, Huxley, and Wallace up to and including contemporary neo-Darwinists. Was creation an accidental occurrence which proceeded through random mutations and natural selection? Or did God create the heaven and the earth which continued in evolution through law and order? This is not a metaphysical question. The correct answer can change the course of civilization.

Darwin's theory influenced biology, genetics, cosmology, paleontolgy, psychology, medicine, political science, sociology, behaviorism, philosophy, theology, education, arts and letters. If Darwin's theory is in error, then all of these disciplines mentioned are in error in varying degrees. Practically all of the text books would have to be rewritten. We can now understand why persistent and conclusive proof, formulated by responsible scientists, that Darwin was indeed in error is not met with enthusiasm by the scientific community. One should not expect that gifted men who so brilliantly, diligently, and laboriously erected a vast structure of knowledge based on Darwin should be expected to welcome the news that Darwin was in error.

What is the alternative? Science certainly looks upon Darwin, Marx, and Freud as mortal men. The concept of infallibility is definitely rejected by science. If our scientists will face this test courageously, all of the sciences will be immeasurably strengthened. It is not easy to be a true scientist. A scientist cannot be measured quantitatively by the number of degrees or accumulation of information. A true scientist should have a measure of courage to correct error and seek the truth—no matter how painful. The alternative is far more painful. To build error upon error is to drift into dogmas, metaphysics, science fiction and mythology.

In the title of this book I denote man as the moral species. In our present Darwinian environment, the term "man" means a member of the species of simians descended from rats. I do not accept this a priori definition of man. My exclusive concern is with the moral species. I do not challenge any science which limits itself to zoological life. But when they include "man," they mean me... and I intend to defend myself. It is my privilege. I regard as impertinent any science which purports to explain and instruct me or my behavior based on the antics of a hungry rat in a cage. Nor will I submit to conclusions about me which are based on research in the life of fruit flies, molluscs, worms, rats, barnacles, or apes. My dignity and destiny are at stake. These are indeed high stakes and I do not propose to surrender my manhood without a struggle.

I include the term destiny in the title. At this present moment only the moral species can be described as posessing a destiny. We alone, among all living creatures, are still in the process of evolution. All other living creatures have reached their destiny. Our lifeline is literally that line which stretches from our point of origin to our point of destination. If we locate our true point of origin we can hold on to this lifeline and reach our destiny in safety and security. If we accept an erroneous point of origin we will inevitably follow the wrong road to extinction. We had better be right. We should examine every promising arrow which points out the road.

We have traversed the road between a rediscovered point of origin to a predicted destiny and have developed a theory of evolution which is in harmony with observed and experienced facts. In our journey we cut across the private domains of many disciplines. This is because we followed a straight line and did not take any detours. We followed the signs. The theory is simple, consistent, and in harmony with revealed universal natural laws. This is an asset in seeking knowledge. The complex and tortuous paths which are followed by existing theories of evolution betray every sign of artificiality. They are full of hastily applied patches and emergency repairs. The road is becoming rougher with each forward motion and is now almost blocked. The theories are leaking badly and can no longer be repaired. It is time to retrace our steps a hundred years and take new soundings.

How much longer dare we risk sailing a leaking ship

of life, travelling on uncharted, storm-tossed seas, guided by a helmsman who steers by chance and commanded by a captain who openly states that he has no point of destination?

Who am I? I am a nervous passenger. Why did I write this book? I want to change the captain and crew.

Scientists cannot absolve their guilt by pointing an accusing finger at the ship of state. Because they, the scientists, plotted the course and gave the directions to the leaders of the future. It is the educators who teach the captains and crews in their youth and advise them in their maturity. Let us look at the record.

It was Darwin who taught and directed us to follow the road of chance, to survive by imitating the laws of the jungle and to reward the bloody victor. His pupils have followed this advice. It was Freud who taught and directed us to follow our sex instinct. This was eagerly adopted in all levels of society. His pupils again followed his teachings. It was Marx who taught and directed us to follow our material instincts. Once again, pupils learned their lessons well. The only thing to be resolved is who gets and uses the products of materialism.

These three prophets mirror our society. Their teachings are the foundation of our educational system. They must accept the guilt for our present chaos. I hope that responsible men will accept the challenge. I hope they will change the captain and the crew and chart a new course which will bring us to our destination safely. I hope they do this, if only to obey the law of self-preservation. We are all men and we will all go down with the ship together.

Origin and Destiny of the Moral Species

I
..."I AM THAT I AM"

This quotation from Exodus is both the beginning of our inquiry and the limitation. Beyond these limits is beyond our conceptual abilities and beyond knowledge. We will use recognized and successful methods of the search for knowledge—a knowledge which may be tested in a laboratory applied to man's own experience, and which will lend itself to experimentation based on predictability. We begin with Creation, and Creation is not conceivable unless we possess knowledge of the Creator. With this knowledge firmly based, many other hitherto unexplainable phenomena will begin to open up a design before our inquiring minds.

It seems a contradiction in terms, but the fact is that if we limit our quest tailored to our own conceptual possibilities, we will find that our knowledge will not be limited—but limitless in scope. We will not exhaust all its potential for an eternity of time. Our first task is to identify the Creator. We can then gain knowledge of the creation of the universe, the nature of matter—the essence of energy, the meaning of life, the purpose of life, and our destiny.

Man on earth is but a speck in a vast, frightening universe. Quantitatively, man is all but a zero. But suppose that man were the only form of life in the universe endowed with the mental and spiritual capacity to identify the Creator in knowledge. If so, and if he succeeds, then he will have performed an incalculable service for the entire universe of matter, mind, and spirit. The heavenly bodies will no longer continue in their endless paths without meaning and purpose. The universe may discover itself, and all life within the universe would then identify itself within this knowledge. Last but not least, man himself may find meaning, purpose, and destiny, and perhaps immortality in a successful search. If man succeeds in this one effort, he will emerge as the dominant creature of the entire universe, and the universe can then be described as revolving around the earth—spiritually. This is why man has never given up this attempt, despite persistent failures; this is why he cannot give up the attempt and why he will continue as long as breath endures. In the absence of evidence to the contrary, man may be the only being in nature that can prove the existence of the universe in reality. This responsibility cannot be taken lightly. He has a responsibility to live up to his potential. The whole universe is waiting. Perhaps this is man's purpose and destiny.

In this quest it is always essential to stay within the bounds of man's own experience. Any departure, however slight, can lead us into unknown and unknowable areas of thought, imagination, and illusion. We must discipline our thoughts far more strictly than is permissible to scientific hypothesis and theory. This is the only safe road in an extremely hazardous exploration. We will be guided by man's own historical experiences.

In human history the most gifted men have wrestled with the problem of man's identity. What is Man? What is reality? What is illusion? Is the universe an illusion conceived only by the mind of man, or is matter the ultimate reality? Was this an exercise in futility, of useless effort—without any practical purpose? To accept such a verdict one would have to classify all the greatest minds who ever lived as fools or dilettantes. To remove these men from the roster of civilization would destroy the heart and soul and the real foundations of society. Perhaps they did not succeed, but their efforts kept alive the hopes, the aspirations, the faith upon which our entire civilization rests. When Descartes proclaimed "I think, therefore I am," the world shook with excitement and relief, believing that man had finally identified himself in the reality of the universe. In the Age of Enlightenment, this was a far more important discovery than the explosion of the atomic bomb. The one brought hope and a resurgence of thought and intellectual groping, a hope that man was on the verge of finding meaning and purpose. The other brought fear and dread. This is only to highlight the importance which men of the Enlightenment attached to the possible discovery and identity of themselves—in knowledge. Of course, the average man and even a child "knew" instinctively and by his own common sense that he was real—in a real universe. So did Descartes. The departure was from instinct, belief, faith—toward knowledge. How can anyone predict the consequences of a universe and man's civilization on earth if *knowledge* of the Creator would supersede instinct and belief?

Descartes almost succeeded, but not quite. Once again there were loopholes in this declaration. Man is still without an identity in *knowledge.* Suppose we apply words from Exodus, "I am that I am," to solve man's identity; and if we succeed we shall have experimental proof in experience that the formula may identify the Creator. Suppose man stated: "I am, therefore I think." Being comes before thinking. And suppose we identify man by his acts of creation in his own civilization. What is Man? I am, therefore I think, reflect, understand. I am, therefore I love, choose between good and evil, do justice, create laws, build institutions. I am, therefore I sing, dance, perform, laugh, cry; write music, poetry, and sagas. I am, therefore I discovered nature's secrets and adapted them for all scientific pursuits. I am, therefore I heal, know compassion and mercy. I am, therefore I build cities and nations. I am, therefore I have produced myriads of things not found in nature.

I have created wheels, engines, wings, electronics, and machines that do my bidding and are created for my purpose and have meaning only for me. When I appeared on earth, civilization did not exist; there was nothing but an amorphous void. I thought and conceived of tools of agriculture, of shelter, and I am the civilization on earth. I created this civilization out of a nonmaterial, spiritual, nonmeasurable, nonobservable, no thing which I call thought. My name is Man. You will know me by what I created, by what I produced. Only if you recognize me and identify me as the creator of civilization will you understand my works. You will not understand the meaning and purpose of the magnificent, elaborate communication system unless you understand that I possess the faculty of transmitting thought through language. You cannot solve the mystery of communication by investigating animal life or my bones. Because I created it to serve *my* purpose. It has meaning only for me. Everything you will see in my created civilization was produced by me. Everything I have ever produced was conceived through a nonmaterial process of thought—to concept, to plan, to design, to production—always for a purpose. You will not find a single thing in my created civilization, from a pin to a generator, that was made by chance.

My machines have no meaning without me. My washing machine has no meaning or purpose without me; it will continue its cyclical movements whether or not there are clothes inside. It is I who put my clothes within it so as to clean them; only then does the machine have meaning. By themselves, all the computers in the world cannot solve a single problem. It is I who solve problems, who understand the questions, who integrate the answers with the aid of computers.

I truly regret that you, the nonhuman universe, possess no faculty of thought—that your faculties are limited by your physical senses. I cannot show you or prove to you the factual existence of thought, I cannot pass the process over into your hands; nor can you see, hear, smell, or touch it. It is beyond your conception; no amount of research will help you. If you hope to understand my civilization, to live in it and enjoy its natural benefits, you must begin by acknowledging man as the creator of this civilization.

Because only through me will you learn the use, purpose, and meaning of this civilization. You will have to obey my rules in order to benefit. You cannot risk using the vast amount of electric energy that you will find here on earth unless you follow instructions precisely. Otherwise you will destroy yourself. These machines require care, fuel, and know-how. I will gradually, through a process of evolution, teach you to adapt your life and needs to these natural machines and institutions. When you learn your lessons well, you can be trusted to use this immense civilization, preserve it, enjoy life and survive. The rules of law must be obeyed if you wish to survive.

This is the laboratory in which we will test our hypothesis. This laboratory is nothing less than the whole of man's created civilization. We stated that we will bring it to the test of man's experience. Man did experience his civilization on earth. We use the term civilization to include all of his cultural, economic, political, and artistic edifices and all his institutions. Though questions about life on other planets are a subject of speculation, no one would suggest that a duplicate of man's civilization will ever be found anywhere else in the universe. No space man should expect to discover Beethoven's symphonies, see a Michelangelo sculpture, read Shakespeare, photograph a Taj Mahal or Empire State Building, or find a second code of man's laws, economic system, or any of his institutions. Civilization on earth is man's creation. It is the *only* process of creation which we can test experimentally.

Man is a very late product of evolution. Since man himself was created, he must be a continuation of a process which began in the dim, unknown, and unknowable period of the beginning. The natural universe indicates continuity in an evolutionary pattern. The electron in a rock is exactly like an electron in a human being. Evolution indicates constant development from previous existing phenomena. Galileo did not cause the earth to move around the sun. He discovered an existing phenomenon. Newton did not endow mass with the force of gravitation; he discovered its laws. It follows with absolute certainty that the process which man utilizes for his own creations is a consequence of his evolutionary development, is an imitation of things found in nature or adapted from existing natural laws which he must first discover. We will examine this process and note how this road will aid us in our quest of the universal creation.

Production is always preceded by thought, a nonmaterial phenomenon. A tool or machine cannot produce thought. Thought can produce a machine or tool. From this observation we must accept the axiom that matter cannot produce nonmaterial phenomena, but nonmaterial phenomena can produce matter. In our experience we know that one cannot produce an object without plan and purpose. The plan may be faulty, the purpose may not be fulfilled or may even be idiotic, but the conception cannot separate an object from its design and purpose. Therefore, the appearance of any created object, whether material, esthetic, or an institution, is proof of the existence of conscious thought, purpose, and plan. The reality of man, of mind, of thought can only be proven by the emergence of a created object.

The scientist will point out that nature produces particles and bodies by means of observed explosions and implosions. They state that these vast "chaotic" events on such a grandiose scale indicate no process of guided or controlled production which we can observe. Take a man with no knowledge of metallurgy into a steel mill. Let him observe the fiery, convulsive behavior of molten metal in a furnace. Is there anything in the furnace which indicates to him guidance or control or order? But take this man to another part of the mill and show him the completed shapes and objects of shining steel. The end product of the fiery furnace is proof of plan, thought, concept, control, and purpose. We look around our earth and observe the completed product. Can such a product result from chaos? We must not permit fancy, imagination, superstition, or magic to get in the way of our own observed experiences. The end product is proof of thought, plan, concept, idea, guidance and control. It cannot be otherwise. Man is justly proud of having brought about the science of cybernetics. It is probably his most sophisticated creation. Let us examine the process by which a computer is created. The computer begins as a chaotic heap of wires and steel and other metals. Taken apart or at the beginning of construction, the wires and metal possess no properties other than their natural state. Construction cannot begin until the idea is first conceived and its purpose decided upon. Though the essence of a computer remains the same, the infinite varieties of size and design take form depending on the purpose and evolution of man's knowledge. It is the result, always, of a thorough and laborious effort of the conscious mind. Only men with the highest degree of specialized knowledge are able to conceive and plan a computer.

When the concept is complete, it first materializes on paper in the form of a plan—an abstract. The plan cannot calculate the position of a space ship—not yet; it is still an abstract computer. The computer is made according to plan. The heart of this plan provides for the creation of instruments within the computer which will enable it to respond to coded electrical messages. The sophistication of its receiving instruments determines its place in the hierarchy of evolution of computers and determines its purpose. Obviously a computer which translates languages will not be used for keeping warehouse inventory. When the computer is built according to plan, its creator knows in advance just what it will do. He can almost calculate its energy requirements and how long it will "live." When the computer is finished, one perceives its highly complex gadgets; but his is not yet the reality of a computer. It is still a mass of expensive junk, still an abstraction.

The impressive heap of metal bulk is then plugged into an electric outlet. The electrical forces race through its interior with the sound of muted power. The bulk of matter shudders momentarily and it is alive with internal momentum—all of its parts are vibrant and humming. What power, what beauty! What has man wrought? It is moving but going nowhere. It needs direction, regulation; it needs a coded message. The secret of this remarkable creature is this: it gets its power from that piece of punched paper inserted into its gullet. True; but something is wrong. The computer keeps repeating the same answers all day and will continue for the rest of its mechanical life. It is man, working far from the scene of his creation, who punches the card in accordance with a built-in code. It is man only who knows why he asked the questions, how to integrate the answers to the whole problem; it is man alone who understands, yet he is the abstract: He is not the computer, nor is he the equivalent of the computer. There is no sensory evidence that he exists at all. He is just a phantom. If you watch a computer work you will not see man; if you disintegrate a computer, the remains will not have man's form. A computer is built, regulated, and directed by man—man is not the building material of a computer. A computer is not built of men—but by man.

Though a computer be as high as the Empire State Building, as broad and long as the Mississippi; though it may utilize the entire electrical output of Boulder Dam, be capable of producing prodigious mathematical tasks, be able to translate all literature into a hundred languages, play chess, write and play music; though it may repair itself, regenerate other computers (we hope with love); though it may move, think, laugh, and cry—if just a single punched card is removed, the entire project collapses, becomes a ludicrous, useless jumble of rusting junk. And that card can be made only by man, its creator, in accordance with man's will and purpose—in accordance with the receiving mechanism which man created in the first place when he built it. It is man who acts upon the computer by means of an invisible communication system of electricity, by means of the physical presence of a coded card that has a meaning only to man.

What is tangible? What is an abstract? Is the computer, with all its size and clanking whirring sounds, tangible or abstract? It seems reasonable and correct to state that the computer in tangible form is only steel and wire; it is abstract until acted upon by the one real force which created the reality of the computer.

Only when man gave the command did the computer begin to "live" in reality. It is possible for a universe consciously created, directed, and regulated under law to develop parts or phenomena within its system that are accidental, purposeless, mechanical, and chaotic. It is impossible and a challenge to sanity and reason to claim that a computer could evolve out of a chaotic, senseless, purposeless, mechanical universe. Though the natural creation was certainly a vast difference in kind from man's creation of civilization, the fundamental process must be similar. It cannot be otherwise unless man created the universe, but this cannot be true because the evolutionary facts prove that he entered the scene after the universe of matter and life already existed in boundless abundance.

A computer or a washing machine has no purpose or meaning of its own. A washing machine will proceed with its cyclical actions whether or not there are clothes inside. A computer does not solve problems; it does not know of any problems. It will behave according to man's built-in instructions. It is meaningless to inquire of a computer what is its purpose and goal. It has none. This is what scientists and philosophers attempt when they consult the products of nature—of nature itself—for answers to transcendental questions. Little wonder they came to the conclusion that the universe and life itself is mechanistic, hopeless and meaningless, and without purpose. To find the answers they will have to communicate with spiritual forces—and to do that, they must first acknowledge the reality of the Creator. With this first step all knowledge will begin to blossom into meaning, purpose and hope will replace despair. How does one attempt communication? Let us once again search man's own experience. How did man communicate with nature? How does science communicate with the physical world, the biological world, and the world of mind and spirit? The method used is to discover the laws of these phenomena, test them according to predictability, and utilize or adapt them for man's creations. Scientists begin by asking questions of nature. They are in no doubt of the existence of nature—of the order in nature, of its laws. Through extremely difficult processes of thought and research, they have slowly uncovered seeming mysteries and brought their findings into the arena of knowledge.

How do artists create their works, composers their symphonies, or poets their cadences? Always by a process of communication. But these creators are highly sensitive receiving mechanisms. A composer will never discover a law of physics, nor will a biologist write music while dissecting plant and animal specimens. We must follow the path of proven methods. We must ask questions within our conceptual possibilities. We must not wait in doubt or be strengthened only by belief, because some questions simply cannot be answered.

Does the physician withhold insulin from diabetic patients because he does not know precisely how it works? Does the physicist withdraw from activity because he does not know the essence of energy or how matter was formed? Does he doubt everything because he does not yet know some things? It is a truism that the gaps in medical knowledge are far greater than their specific areas of knowledge. Yet a man places his well-being and his very life in the hands of a surgeon. This is because of the things they do know, however limited, that are far more important, far more decisive than the superstition and magic of witch doctors or alchemists or astrologers. Knowledge is the only firm base for progress in all of man's endeavors. Even if we know nothing else, it is no small thing to possess knowledge of the Creator. Other knowledge will follow. To be petulant and demand instant knowledge of the most difficult of all intellectual disciplines is to continue in the darkness of doubt and ignorance.

"In the beginning God created the heaven and earth. And the earth was without form, and void; and darkness was upon the face of the deep. And the spirit of God moved upon the face of the waters. And God said: 'Let there be light.''

There can be no sensible beginning of the reality of the universe unless we mean the appearance of matter and mass. Cosmologies which begin with explosions or implosions already accept the existence of energy and the laws of physics. The particles of matter, of mass, of light had to possess characteristics which enabled them to develop forms. Whatever existed prior to the appearance of energy, matter, mass, and their precise laws, we cannot know. We cannot ask and receive a sensible reply to the question, "What is the nature of matter—what is it made of?" Because if matter is made "of" some material thing—whether one calls this ether or something else—the question arises: "What is ether made of?" If matter is made "of" energy, then what is energy made of? How can a nonspatial product convert itself into mass? No matter how much energy or force of energy may be accumulated, it still does not project in space. Einstein's famous $E=MC^2$ can be understood only as a quantitative measurement indicating the quantity of energy released when matter disintegrated or the quantity of energy used in producing a given quantity of mass. Matter is not made "of" energy; it is produced by forces of energy. To repeat, nothing in our own experience has ever been produced without the prior utilization of thought, concept, idea, will, purpose, and law. If the nonmaterial energy produced matter, what is the essence of energy? We can only reach the borders of our conceptual abilities.

We know that energy is not a material thing. Then it must be a nonmaterial thing, otherwise we would be compelled to state that energy is nothing. We know that a nonmaterial process can produce material things but a material process cannot produce nonmaterial phenomena. We know that energy exists, because we use it all the time. If it exists, we know it was produced, for nothing can come into being otherwise. We also know how material things are produced by a nonmaterial process because we do it in our creations. Thus we know that energy was conceived of an idea, took form in thought, propelled by a will, guided and controlled by law, and always for a purpose in accordance with plan. Therefore we know that the Creator produced energy. We cannot know the technology. We can know, to the same degree that a primitive "knows," that man produced a space ship, exploded an atomic bomb, communicates directions to a satellite 90,000 miles away from earth—yet not know *how*. Actually, how many men know how radio, television, or an airplane is produced. Men may use the telephone and yet know nothing of electronics. If they were to spend a lifetime of study and research in only one small part of the science of man they would know only a fragment. They persist in using different guidelines for the acquisition of knowledge in the universal creation when the only road to knowledge is the familiar one of man's own experiences. Energy forces are not the building blocks of matter—they are the forces which form the building blocks of matter. Matter is not constructed *of* energy—matter is constructed *by* energy.

Physicists have identified four kinds of potential energy associated with gravitational force, electromagnetic force, strong nuclear force, and weak nuclear force. The present-day philosophy of physics is that all matter is created of (consists of) elementary particles such as electrons, protons, and neutrons. These particles are bound together by the four different kinds of forces associated with potential energy. Forces have been merely inferred by some physicists, and motion is nothing in itself; yet the combination of these two results in work, which is something very real. Work is the one physical reality that cannot be argued away. We cannot argue away the very real fact that the universe was produced, through work, by various kinds of energy ... and work—production—is always preceded by thought, plan, concept, will, law and purpose.

Kinetic energy depends on the mass and velocity of a body. It can be observed, utilized, and measured. Potential energy gives no sign of its existence. One cannot ascertain which piece of iron has the potential magnetic force of energy. A lump of coal or liquid gasoline or gunpowder does not reveal its immense store of potential energy; yet kinetic energy, observable and in motion, can only become materialized through the release of stored or potential energy. The measured quantity of kinetic energy thus released can never be of a greater quantity than the silent and unobserved potential energy at rest within a body. Even in a perfect system a lump of coal or a gallon of gasoline cannot produce more kinetic energy than what existed in its potential. Nor can a mind produce observable and materialized phenomena to a greater degree than its potential. One can put a gorilla in the intellectual environment of a university for many generations, but it will never write a play, deliver an address, discuss philosophy, or create a machine. The pigeons in St. Marks Square will never appreciate art or build an altar. The creatures in Walden Pond can never approach the potential mind of Thoreau even if they lived there another billion years. Environment itself produces nothing. The potential energy of a mind confronted by an existing material environment does produce or create—always within the limitation of the potential energy of the mind. We, from our own experience, know the vast difference in mind potential between lower beings and man. We know those differences among various civilizations and advanced cultures. We know the vast differences in mind potential in children of the same parents. Isn't it reasonable to accept the existence of a far greater mind in the universe, greater than the distance between a speck and man? We are almost convinced that higher intellects exist somewhere in outer space, in the form of little men with feelers on their brows. We almost accept this fancy even though we have never seen any evidence of this superior intellect in work or production.

How would we ascertain the quality of a Martian intellect? By an I.Q. test? Would we assume that his mathematics, science, and philosophy are similar to ours, though his environment is totally different. Language would not help. We cannot know whether Martians have developed a superior or at least a different form of communication, perhaps a form of thought transmission. We would only recognize their degree or kind of intellectual or mind potential by what they produced: a superior space ship, superior engineering, superior communication system, and mainly by the condition of their creatures. Do they live in peace? Then their political system is superior. Are they happy, content, productive, and creative? This would be evidence of a superior civiliation. Yet we refuse to accept the same standards of proof in acknowledging the existence of a Creator. We ignore materialized, productive, orderly evidence, and we grope for the terms of infinity and eternity, which are beyond our comprehension. Time and space are human categories which do not exist as universal entities. The same intellects who label man as an insignificant, meaningless speck in the universe, different in degree but not in kind from animal and even vegetable life, insist that unless the Creator can be apprehended in man's limited mind potential, then he does not exist in actuality. They want it both ways: man is nothing; man is everything.

Potential forces of energy may lead us to clues of creation and evolution. They are not limited to particles of matter. Potential energy may also explain biological materialization of life and mind or spirit. While four kinds of potential forces have been identified in matter, we may find many more kinds of potential forces of energy associated with other phenomena. Once again, for emphasis: potential forces are not recognized by what they are; they are nonmaterial things; they are recognized by what they do. In their interaction with kinetic energy, they work and produce observable things. There is no such thing as a "chemical force." These are reactions of atoms entirely under the control of electrical forces between electrons and protons in the atom. All production or materialization is therefore an electrical process. All electrical processes are set in motion by the interaction of kinetic and potential energy. Therefore creation was an act producing material things from nonmaterial potential energy forces through measurable and observable kinetic energy.

A particle of matter in the form of a chemical compound has no life potential. Its potential to materialize into a specific kind of plant, animal, or man is guided, controlled, and directed by a life energy force within the nucleus. This potential life energy force is limited to the production of a specific form of life and nothing else. The potential life energy force in an acorn will produce an oak tree and nothing else. The potential energy forces are activated into the motion of kinetic energy by the necessary ingredients of soil, nourishment, water, and sun. Advanced knowledge of agriculture simply extracts more from potential energy in the same manner that better engines extract more power from a gallon of fuel. They cannot go beyond its original potential energy.

How do we know that a life force of potential energy exists in living matter? Only because we can synthesize an inorganic colloidal compound to equal an organic compound. The potential energy in inorganic matter has reached the limit of its potential; it can produce no further. The living cell will continue to grow and show all signs of living activity, limited by its life energy potential. All nature—the natural universe which we can know—is the sum total of created potential energy forces in accordance with plan. The universe of reality was already in existence in concept before the first movement of kinetic energy appeared to form the first particles of matter. This concept existed in the "mind" of the Creator and it had to be the Creator who could command the beginning of motion: "Let there be light—and there was light."

There was a piece of land in New York City bounded by 34th Street, 32nd Street, and Fifth and Sixth Avenues. The Empire State Building did not exist yet. Men decided to erect a building on the site. They hired an architect. The Empire State Building existed in the mind of the architect before the first shovel of soil was excavated. The architect had to know and plan the entire structure in all its details before the foundation was laid. Moreover, the architect had to know the purpose of the building before he could plan. How many stores, how many offices, how many people would be engaged in work; what kind of work; when would they arrive and when would they leave. All of this knowledge was required in order to plan for elevators, heat, light, air-conditioning, and electrical outlets. The resulting plans and specifications were the potential force of energy. Nothing existed on this piece of land except the concept and potential. The architect could have called a press conference on this piece of land and prophesied accurately all the details of this building to the assembled reporters. The building would have so many elevators, would be 102 stories high, would accommodate a work force of so many people.... Was this an act of magic? We know that these things came about as a result of extremely difficult creative processes.

Universal creation does not mean the sudden appearance of spatial bodies, of animal or plant life or man. These are the products of development in evolution. Creation and evolution are entirely different processes. Creation is the concept, the plan, the potential. Evolution is the materialization of degrees of the whole potential depending on many factors which we will discuss later. But evolution could never function nor could anything be materialized without the blueprint. This is true of the Empire State Building; how infinitely more true in the creation of nature and its subsequent evolution. In this context there is no contradiction in the biblical version of cosmogony.

There is no contradiction between creation and evolution. This hypothesis carries with it enormous and extremely important meaning for man. Here on earth we know that plant and zoological life have reached the limit of their evolutionary development. Only man at present is still in the process of evolving. Who knows what his potential is? Or even if there is a limit in the sense of human categories. If he is made in the image of God, then his potential is...? He cannot discover his potential by casting himself in the image of a rat or reducing himself to a physical zero in the immense mass of the universe. Nor will his advance in evolution be automatic, as a result of chance mutations. Evolution in any species ends when a species has either reached the limits of its potential or makes no further effort to reach its full potential. Only then does evolution halt and nature produces things automatically—through mechanistic processes. This is what we do in our own civilization. We bring a product to the highest point of its potential, that is, perfect it—then we mass-produce it. When we create a newer object, the older model is discarded. Man would become an automatic species if he did not continually strive for perfection in evolution.

Matter and Natural Laws

Matter is created, produced, activated, and guided in accordance with precise plan through the medium of various energy forces. The one certain guideline in the continuity of evolution is the materialization from less complex to more complex forms. Production according to plan is always accompanied by purpose. The purpose is known to the creator of a particular product. We know this too, from our own experience. Who else but man decided on the purpose, meaning, and destiny of his created objects, from pencil to clock to computer? It is man who decided to divide time into seconds, minutes, hours, according to his earthly environment. A clock transferred to Mars or Venus would have no apparent meaning there. With sufficient research and intelligent deduction, provided life on another planet had these properties, beings could "discover" the concept or process of keeping time as related to Earth. Without such intelligence and effort, the time objects would be meaningless for life on Mars or Venus. Since anything which has no meaning or purpose must be classified as a mechanistic chance occurrence, the conclusions would be erroneous, though logical. The only way to arrive at truth would be for the beings to discover and acknowledge the reality of man as creator of the clock, then with further research everything else would become clear.

It is also a fact that man's created civilization proceeded from the simple to the more complex. The first automobile was little more than of horse-and-wagon design with motor replacing horse. Even the rate of speed was hardly more than the speed of a horse in gallop. The automobile then "evolved" by slow, imperceptible changes until we now operate complex and beautiful vehicles. The older models, unable to compete, became extinct through a process of natural selection; but this selection was not automatic; it was inevitable. But it was the choice and acts of man which resulted in new models and the inevitable obsolescence of the old. Yet many basic parts survived and became an essential form for all automobiles. For example, the wheel not only remains a basic part of all automobiles, but for all kinds of locomotive vehicles. The wheel still is used for oxcarts in some primitive villages, and is also the basic component of more complex vehicles, timing devices, and machinery. It is extended throughout civilization, just as the eye as an organ of vision occurs in life forms. The fact that automobile is mass-produced and that many of its parts are produced through automation is not proof that it appeared by chance—mechanistically. The advent of a product always means it was produced—and production must always originate with concept, plan, and purpose.

Nor will man's civilization endure if, as creator, he abandoned his creations to mechanistic laws. If construction workers convinced themselves that they no longer needed architects and engineers, or if men generally tried to eliminate thought, ideas, concepts, and creation on the assumption that technology could continue mechanistically, it would not be long before civilization would begin to run down and ultimately disappear. We have experienced this process when men who had no ability to create, or who did not understand creative processes—like the barbaric tribes—took over an existing civilization. We know what happened in Rome and we know what happened more recently in the Congo. When men do not recognize or acknowledge the Creator—either the creators of civilization or the Creator of nature—chaos results. This we know from experience.

Natural laws are neither chance occurrences nor mechanistic. The mechanism was built into the product just as the mechanism was built into a watch. The natural laws of the timepiece are predictable, observable, and mechanistic. Its second hand will rotate precisely; its cycle of sixty seconds will move the minute hand, and in sixty minutes the hour hand will have moved to the next digit. It will continue as exactly as the quality of materials developed for this purpose allows. Actually, the more perfect the timing on a watch, the greater appreciation and admiration for its maker. One does not worship a fine timepiece; one has faith and trust in the company that made it.

The natural law of a piece of steel with a sharp blade is to penetrate or cut a softer object. A razor blade can cut a jugular vein and mutilate flesh. When such a blade is locked into a special holder it is now no longer a sharp-edged piece of steel; it is now a safety razor. With this transformation in form, the natural laws of the separate blade no longer apply in the new product. The razor will now glide over flesh harmlessly, removing only excess hair. This physical natural law of the safety razor is automatic, mechanistic, can never change, and can always be relied upon to perform its task. Because this is its "law," men use the safety razor without fear. Similarly a compound of hydrogen and oxygen no longer has the properties of either gas. It is now water, with its own characteristics or natural laws. The natural laws or properties of any product in nature or in civilization are a result of a creative process. When the prototype or model is finally perfected, the work of kinetic energy forces is then brought into play in the process of mass production.

As our probes into space go farther and there continues to be no response or evidence of human forms beyond our planet, the chances become less that mere extension of distance will bring such evidence. It may well be that man on earth is unique. The fact that he created a watch, razor blade, or even a space ship is of no conceivable relationship to the creation of matter and life. What is important—what is decisive in our context—is that man is a product of creation and that he also *created* things while the rest of the universe was merely created. This is the key word, "creation," not mechanism or quantity. It has been stated that if our civilization lost 200,000 key men in the field of creative ability, our civilization would grind to a halt. This process of man's creation is a worthy experimental laboratory in which to explore the Creation. In the Biblical version the creation of matter was accompanied by a command: "Let there be light." the creation of life was accompanied by a blessing: "Be fruitful and multiply." The creation of man was accompanied by the warning: "Do not eat the fruit of the tree of knowledge-lest ye die."

This essay has tried to avoid both philosophy and value judgments. Not with complete success, we admit. The subject is of such magnitude that this evasion of value judgments or philosophy leaves tremendous gaps in our exposition. We do not possess the ability to enter these areas of thought and we doubt that any man can express a new word, a new thought, or idea which has not already been recorded in the immense theological and philosophical literature of man's recorded history. We are attempting a search for knowledge—the kind of knowledge which states that in accordance with laws of physics, a man who will jump from a ten story building will be killed. Why nature so created man that he will die by falling or jumping is not the province of the physicist. We know that air-breathing animals will drown when submerged in water. Why the Creator did not equip animals with two kinds of breathing apparatus is not the legitimate area of the search for knowledge by scientists. Why viruses, microbes, and germs? Why tornadoes, earthquakes, and hurricanes? Why are the wicked rewarded and the righteous punished? These are extremely important inquiries.

Men learned to adapt themselves to the natural world only after they grasped its workings in knowledge. They fashioned parachutes so that a man can jump safely from high altitudes. They concocted drugs and medicines to overcome the virus, germ and microbe. They invented a breathing apparatus which enables them to remain under water for extended periods of time. When we will grasp the process of universal creation, acknowledge and "know" the Creator—learn His laws which direct and guide the spirit and mind of man—man can then fashion his environment to conform with these laws, adapt them for his benefit in terms of peace, happiness, and justice. This will not only enable us to survive, but to be fruitful and multiply, to widen areas of knowledge—to evolve into our potential, and perhaps glimpse immortality.

A one-sided evolution of our own technology will

end in disaster and probably extinction. Lawless beings will not be permitted to roam through space, especially when that creature is one with a well-documented criminal record of mass extermination.

And God said: "Let the earth put forth grass, herb yielding seed, and the fruit tree yielding fruit of its kind, whose seed is in itself, upon the earth." The first stage of evolution was completed. The forms of matter had reached a level of complexity which enabled it to respond to the vital forces of energy associated with life. The transformation in material form was one of degree, not kind. The structure of matter was the same in both the living and nonliving matter. The living materials were more complex forms of the same basic material. The force of energy associated with living activity, or what we will call life energy, was a transformation in kind, not degree. "Transformed" should not be used in describing an energy process. Because energy has no form, any change in the kind of energy force present in any matter would only be known and recognized by what it does. This new "matter" was different in kind, because it was living matter. It is a fact that any material, from rock to man, must possess within its structure a force of energy, in the form of a detectable electric charge.

According to modern physics, "There is no such thing as a "chemical force." Such terms are simply left over from the days when people did not realize that the reactions between atoms were entirely under the control of electrical forces between the electrons and protons in the atoms. Here we have a scientific statement that atoms act and react upon matter. Since there is no discoverable difference in construction of matter between living and nonliving substances, and in any case their activity is the result of electrical forces, it is certain in the strictest scientific sense that the energy forces associated with living activity are different in kind (qualitative) from energy forces associated with nonliving activity.

The difference in complexity in various forms of matter means simply that a more complex or more sophisticated structure of matter is a finer or superior instrument of detection. As matter evolves into more complex forms it is enabled to detect, apprehend, perceive, and know more advanced kinds of life phenomena through the communications system of existing electrical forces. A simply constructed radio using crystals for receiving can detect radio waves within a very limited area. A more sophisticated instrument, like the one built into an Explorer rocket aimed at Mars, was able to detect a message from 92,000,000 miles away and to act on this message. Radio waves exist and radio waves have always existed. Marconi did not create radio waves; he built an instrument to detect their presence. This is the logical and scientific way to explain "ambigenesis," continuity in evolution, and evolution itself. There is no reason why we must continue to build our theories on flimsy evidence, even if those theories are the result of massive documentation. We should appreciate the efforts that went into documentation, but judge the truth more heavily on evidence based on experience—our own experience.

The earth, its material structure completed, was pregnant with the seeds of potential life energy. The earth emerged from the fiery furnace as a magnificently designed planet qualified to support life, its atmosphere protected by clouds of gases to resist lethal penetration of the sun's rays and other forms of radiation, its surface replete with water, the essential catalyst of all living activity. Its surface cooled, its rhythm of seasons, rotation, winds and tides controlled by built-in laws—everything was in readiness. The rains came, and the seeds containing their life-energy forces broke through the earth to continue their embryonic growth in the incubator of the sun, nourished by air and water.

For the sake of convenience and clarity we have used the term "forces of energy," which we have borrowed from the physicists. We transposed their definition as we entered the stage of living activity by simply calling it life forces of energy. In describing "kinds" of energy we must state our own definition. In our definition there are no *kinds* of energy. Energy is the force which produces various kinds of work. Electricity is the same force which works to produce a multitude of things. Heat, light, and power are different kinds of work which are produced under the direction of man. Electricity itself knows nothing, produces nothing. Uncontrolled, it will kill men and destroy cities. We conceive of energy forces as operating and working to produce different kinds of things under the direction and control of the Creator in accordance with the natural system of the universe.

Therefore, forces of energy cannot be identified or separated in categories by examining their form, shape, or properties. They differ only in what they do. Not to understand or have knowledge of the role of energy in the construction of the universe is to know nothing. Everywhere we are faced with insoluble problems.

What is energy? It is not a material thing. What separates matter from living activity? Not a material thing. What separates vegetation from the beginnings of zoological life? Not a material thing. What separates the lowest form of human life from the highest forms of zoological life? What is mind? How did creation begin? All vital questions which now leave enormous gaps in our knowledge are connected by nonmaterial things. Yet we keep searching for material missing links.

These nonmaterial things created our own civilization and produced our vaunted industrial wealth. It is no exaggeration to state that without knowledge of these nonmaterial things it is we who know nothing. When we know the source of these nonmaterial things, we will know *everything.* This is not a play on words. It is a practical, necessary and a vital addition to our store of knowledge. This addition will explain everything; without it, nothing can be explained. We have our choice. We can continue to construct on our own imagination and fancy. We can continue to try to solve these problems through metaphysics or philosophy. We can continue to evade these questions in physics, mathematics, and all the related sciences. We can continue to tread the path of evolutionary theories which we have never experienced in our evolution and which no one has ever witnessed or proved. Or—all of our strenuous efforts can become beacons of light which will illuminate the ladder of life, if we begin with the knowledge of the Creator as the one reality. Otherwise everything is illusion.

It must have been quite an event—this emergence of life on earth. The earth, about that period, was covered with flowers. The mind of man cannot conceive the appearance of an entire earth covered with indescribable shapes, colors, and heavy fragrance of flowers. We cannot conceive this scene even though we know of many varieties of flowers, have cultivated them, smelled them, and placed them in many beautiful arrangements. Only the "mind" of the Creator could possibly conceive of an idea of flowers and cover the whole earth with such dazzling beauty—a celebration so to speak, heralding the birth of life on earth.

This appearance of a celestial symphony of beauty was interpreted by Darwin and the evolutionists as simply a consequence of sexual selection. The flowers produced dazzling shapes, colors, and fragrance so that they could attract insects who would act as the carriers of their pollen. An entire volume has been devoted to the proposition that beauty as such does not exist, that it is all a process of sexual selection. Now, beauty as such is a human concept. Men, like animals, possess sensory organs. They can smell, touch, see, hear, and taste, though in different degrees. Though the apprehension of beauty does please the senses, the concept of beauty as developed by man is a far more involved process than simple sensory perception. When one is hungry the smell of food is a pleasant sensation; it is not beauty.

When one is thirsty in a desert and sees a muddy pool of water, it is pleasant to the senses; but it is not beauty. When one hears the approach of an emergency police car while trapped in an automobile, it is pleasant, it is not beauty. When one is sexually attracted, considerations of beauty are secondary; it is simply a satisfaction of instinctual needs.

The concept of beauty has been laboriously developed by man in his ascent toward higher forms of existence. Great poets, artists, philosophers, and theologians have expended their creative abilities and dedicated their lives to bringing the concept of beauty to ever higher standards in order to bring beauty into an otherwise drab and difficult existence. They saw beauty in the simplest abstracts of line, color, and form; they saw beauty in all of nature. They saw beauty in charm, personality, and spirit. They worked to materialize beauty in architecture, fabrics, paintings, music, sculpture, language—in myriads of material forms. We consider Leonardo DaVinci as a great connoisseur of beauty. It is said that he was reluctant to paint nudes because the sexual attraction interfered with his perception of beauty.

How can evolutionists dare transfer this human attribute, this divine concept, to insects in pursuit of sexual attraction? Would not the simple color green in a desolate landscape of brown earth be sufficient to attract insects? Are we to believe that insects are so discriminating in their perception of beauty that they require a blaze of colors which even a Van Gogh went mad trying to capture. Would not the simple fragrance of grass be sufficient to lure insects, or are we to believe that their sense of smell is so highly developed that they require a paradise of fragrance? We rather think that bees would extract nectar from any source because bees need the nectar to satisfy their instincts for survival. Nor have we ever observed dogs in mating stop to admire each other's beauty. This method of transferring human concepts to lower forms of life in order to bring man down to the lower forms of existence is a process leading to *The Descent of Man.* It is a valid method for Walt Disney, not for scientists.

Why is this so important to man? Because this theory influenced the thoughts of generations of men and led man to build error upon error. No less a genius than Sigmund Freud was influenced by Darwinism and came to the conclusion that all of man's creation, his entire civilization, was the result of the sublimation of the sex instinct. Freud went Darwin one better: not only beauty, but everything in civilization can be traced to the sublimation of sex. Has this ever been tested scientifically? Why don't psychonanalysts organize a colony of dogs, forcibly "sublimate" their sex instincts, and prove to man that this suppression will result in dogs' becoming intellectual, rational, moral creatures that can begin building a kind of dog civilization.

Where have they shown any evidence that primitive men ever practice continence? Is celibacy known among aborigines? Isn't it a fact that the less civilized, the less intellectual and moral peoples are slaves to their animal instincts? Isn't it a fact that men first developed characteristics of a higher form of spiritual existence and then were able to dominate their animal instincts? Today millions of people on couches are getting advice and guidance for elevating their lives from a philosophy originally based on the transference of human concepts to animal life. Our advice to these troubled souls: You are humans, not animals. Get off the couches and get on your knees—in prayer.

"I Am Thy God Who Brought You Out of Egypt."

We must not be led too far astray in comparisons between man's creation in civilization and the creation of the universe. Of course these represent vast and inconceivable differences in kind (qualitative). The best that we can do is to discover a process. Philosophers sensing a master plan of the natural creation have attempted to emulate the natural system by developing their own complete systems for man's civilization.

The Indian philosophers of the closed society, the historical systemizers, in effect wanted to substitute their own master plan and to replace the plan of the Creator. Theologians, on the other hand, also sensing the existence of such a Divine plan, countered with concepts of fate and predestination.

Let us examine the Declaration of Independence, the United States Constitution, and the Bill of Rights. If we mean by predestination that as long as American citizens obey the guidelines and laws of these documents they will remain a free and democratic nation—that this will be their fate—then it is correct. If we mean that the master plan governing American civilization limits, plans, and directs every action of its citizens and places them in permanent caste systems, then it is incorrect. This is the aim of a closed society. The universal master plan displays every material and observable evidence of an open society. The first of the Ten Commandments illustrates this point. "I am thy God who brought you out of Egypt." Heading the

Constitution of the Ten Commandments is the promise of freedom.

As we leave the first stage of evolution and enter life, the difference in kind manifests itself with freedom of choice. The ability to create is not possible without freedom of choice. This is the key word which we should follow in the examination of life. It is the word which makes evolution of life possible. It is the word which gives meaning and purpose to all of life's phenomena, beginning with reproduction, sensations, response, up to the spiritual senses.

The sound of thunder, the colors of vegetation, the textures and odors of nature existed before the appearance of life. Life did not create sound, color, odor, and texture. Life discovered them. This discovery or perception was nevertheless an act of secondary creation. It was the creation of instruments or organs of sensation which detected the primary created phenomena. It is this duality which determines the true existence of anything. It is in this confrontation with life that the universe reveals itself. It reveals itself to whom? To what? The universe reveals itself to life. Not to the matter of life—but to the "mind" of life. Not only to the "mind" of man, but to the "mind" of all living creatures. It reveals itself to the degree which creatures of life develop the complexity or sophistication of this "mind" which enables life to perceive or discover ever higher phenomena already existing in nature. As the "mind" develops, it produces, directs, and guides the construction of life organs in accordance with its integrated choice through creative acts.

This dual process is recognized in scientific

disciplines and it is called by different names, performing different functions. It is the duality of energy forces which result in work—of production. This is the technology of the natural production. In physics it is the action and response of kinetic energy with potential energy which produces work resulting in the material forms. In biology there is a second kind of duality which results in living activity. This is the action and response between the inherited forces of life energy with the existing environment.

With man there is an additional kind, or third duality. This is the action and response between the energy forces associated with spirit and the existing spiritual environment. Matter cannot respond to energy forces of life because it does not possess the receiving apparatus with which to perceive its existence. Vegetation, and zoological forms cannot respond to spiritual forces of energy, because they do not have the required receiving apparatus. Only man possesses all three forces of energy.

When a man loses his spiritual energy forces either through degeneration or complete spiritual corruption, he still continues to function as any zoological creature. We might call this the death of the spirit, but he continues to respond to life energy forces. When a man loses his life energy forces we call this death, because life activity has ceased. At the point of biological death, matter has not changed. It is exactly the same as in life. Matter vanishes completely when it is dissociated from its energy forces. Let us return to this sequence of events. What is left when energy is dissociated from matter—the same force which gave matter its forms of existence—the nonmaterial, nonspatial energy? What remains when life energy forces depart from living matter—the same forces which produced life, and life forces of energy, nonmaterial and nonspatial? What remains when spiritual forces of energy depart from the living man—the spiritual forces of energy which produced the spirit?

Not long ago scientists taught that matter is indestructible. The atom was the foundation of mass. The Atomic Age exploded this theory. Now we know that only energy is indestructible and this means all forces of energy. One can very easily be led into mysticism, but it is our intention to avoid this avenue of inquiry.

Man as creator of his civilization can and does know the meaning and purpose of the material and nonmaterial products of his creations. This must be qualified, however. Not all men know the purpose and meaning of the creative products emanating from artistic, philosophical, economic, or scientific disciplines. It is difficult, if not impossible, for a physicist or mathematician to explain a formula, law, equation, or theory in the language of laymen. But any man who enters an airplane and flies to his destination within close proximity of the predicted schedule knows and experiences the end product of an original theory. He has experienced the results of pure and applied science and mathematics, of engineering and production techniques, plus the enormus organization of laws that guide and direct his flight.

Even this must be qualified. An animal which is being transported by air will not perceive the creative processes of man nor understand the meaning and purpose of this airplane. This does not mean that man did not create the airplane or that it has no meaning or purpose. It is beyond the conceptual capabilities of an animal. We must keep these limitations in mind when we explore the primary creation of the Creator. We did not witness or experience these events. We must also keep these limitations in mind when we explore the lowest rung of the secondary creation which began with the first appearance of life. We did not witness or experience this event either. We did experience and witness our own creation, and because we did we can discover the process. We must not conclude that the visible, material end products which we observe in the universe, or nonmaterial, nonvisible phenomena which we feel or detect with our mind, have no meaning or purpose or came into being by chance. It may only be our conclusion for lack of knowledge or because the concept is beyond our comprehension. We may fly through the heavens in a space craft with as little concept of the meaning of heaven as a horse being transported through the atmosphere of earth.

The meaning and purpose of the primary creation is known to the Creator. As life continues to evolve by means of its secondary creations, and as life perceives, detects understands and captures in knowledge wider vistas of the primary creation, life itself becomes more clearly defined and its meaning and purpose revealed. Higher forms of life can be evaluated and measured by the quality of instruments they possess which enable it to acquire such knowledge. Knowledge of creation leads to knowledge of creators. As life acquires ever higher knowledge of the primary Creation, its potential is to acquire knowledge of the Creator. This is its direction and goal. The definition of life would then be: Life is the force to which and by which the existing universe reveals itself.

The materialization of life on earth did not begin with the material of vegetation or biological forms. A flower, insect, or tree did not appear as if by magic. Material forms of life were preceded by the form of a seed. The form of a specific seed was preceded by the form of genes within that seed. The material form of genes was preceded by an energy force associated with life. This energy has no form. With the additional presence of life energy forces in matter, there were now two potential energy forces incorporated in the material of living creatures. The potential of the life energy was limited in every fixed species of plant and animal life. They could choose and evolve only within the limits of their potential. Where did this life energy originate? It originated from the same source as other forces of energy. When we discover the source of one, we will discover the source of all. Since energy forces are nonmaterial and nonspatial, the creation of the entire universe could be completed in accordance with plan, yet there would be no evidence of form or mass.

Just as we try to avoid philosophy, metaphysics, and theology, we also try to avoid discussing various sciences. And for the same reason. We are not qualified scientists, and there already exists a great body of literature on evolution. The guidelines of our own created civilization helped us follow a process of creation of matter. Since man has never produced life in his own civilization, these guidelines are no longer valid in our examination of the process of the creation of life and its evolution.

The forms of life which have been materialized in matter are the result of work or production by energy forces. In order to trace the evolution of life we must examine the work of energy forces. Reproduction is the process of producing something already in existence. As we peel off layer after layer of existing forms of life we must eventually disclose the beginning of life. We cannot avoid this and still make any sense of subsequent events. At some stage life manifested itself in reproduction. Only a force of energy associated with life could vitalize a process of reproduction from an advanced and complex compound of matter to cellular activity. It was the duality of energy forces of life and the energy forces of the environment which produced sensation. Light, heat, odors, sound—these phenomena are all transferred by energy forces. We know them as waves of sound, heat, light, and odor. These waves which carried these phenomena existed prior to the appearance of life. In a universe empty of life, there existed no instruments to detect the environment. The waves of energy which carried the knowledge of the environment were a one-directional communication system. With the appearance of life, the receiving instruments began to evolve which received the message of the universe. The universe revealed itself to life through this system of communication.

The basis for identifying knowledge and memory as energy forces is that they exhibit the same characteristics of all other known and acknowledged forces of energy. They are nonmaterial and nonspatial. Their presence can be observed only by what they produce—not by what they are. The accumulated knowledge and memory of an Einstein does not materialize in an enlarged structure of the brain. Many men of primitive tribes have been found with larger brains than exist in a genius of the most advanced human beings. Yet scientists who adhere to a seemingly irrevocable evaluation that all life processes are chemical and material in essence simply ignore the fact that the energy forces of a genius produce vastly superior objects than the energy forces of a primitive. Once again the evidence of the end product escapes their attention. They persist in subjecting brain tissue to microscopic tests for proof of superiority. The products of an Einstein do not seem to merit sufficient scientific proof.

We have no quarrel with facts of science, we vigorously oppose the evaluation of these facts. This theory is not contrary to known scientific facts as documented by evolutionists. In this limited area there is nothing new in our postulates; one might state there is only a difference in semantics. It is true that we have not brought out new facts. It is not true that the difference is only in terms of language used.

The language of scientists defines evolution in terms of nature. It is nature which is responsible for selection, evolution, development, and the manifestation of life processes. When biologists are confronted with a perplexing and inexplicable fact, they answer usually that it is the work of nature. Nature works, it seems. It is no accident that literature has developed such terms as Dame Nature; the Greeks mythologized nature and animism deified nature. There is a strong implication that nature knows all, sees all, and possesses volition. Complex chemical processes which elude the searching eyes of great chemists are described as the "work of nature." The inconceivable knowledge required of the technology of manufacturing eyes becomes the work of nature. When pressed to identify any product in nature which displays such enormous gifts, the semantics are changed. It now becomes the environment of nature. This is correct provided we know the definition of nature. All we have achieved is to build an image of environment on the previously accepted image of nature as being all-wise and all-knowing. This is an evasion, not an explanation. It is building error upon a foundation of error.

It is correct to state that in developed nations man lives in an environment of civilization. It is correct to state that such an environment builds or develops men of stature in the arts, sciences, politics, and industry. It is also correct to state that all products, from a radio to spacecraft, are produced in an environment of civilization. From this it becomes permissible to state that civilization builds, develops, produces, and is all-knowing and all-wise. All of these language definitions make sense because we know the definition of civilization. We know that men created this civilization out of great effort of his mind and spirit, and at an enormous cost. We know it was not an automatic growth due to chance. It is this fundamental knowledge of the processes of civilization which permits the use of poetic language; but if one removes man from civilization or man becomes extinct, then what does civilization as a semantic term mean? Exactly nothing. Then civilization knows nothing, does nothing, produces nothing.

The terminology of nature makes complete sense when one has knowledge of the Creator of nature. It is the Creator who organized nature, produces and directs it through various forces of energy, and these energy forces work and produce in accordance with concept and plan for a purpose. It is desirable and even necessary to use the terminology of nature and natural forces. We must only understand and have knowledge of the Creator of this nature and natural forces.

How important is this to man? It is important enough to have been, and continues to be, the main cause of his agonies. Through sophisticated and cynical intellectual and philosophical deduction, man removed the Creator from His creation. These same men quickly moved into this vacuum and put on the mantle of power, dominating all creation including the lives of men. Thus followed concepts of divine right of kings and tyrants of all descriptions. This resulted in closed societies with rigid caste systems, of which India is a prime example. These philosophers of India decided in advance—to eternity—which groups of humans would become warriors, scientists, philosophers, leaders, garbage collectors, and prostitutes. The kings, conquerors, and adventurers decided that they could control and dominate the universe, at least to the extent that they could conquer by force. And today we already have new pretenders. They will create life; they will decide in advance the characteristics of all life through genetic manipulation. New terrors and agonies await man unless he overthrows these pretenders and acknowledges the Creator. They must be challenged in the words written in Book of Job: "Gird up now thy loins like a man; for I will demand of thee, and answer thou unto me. Where wast thou when I laid the foundations of the earth? Declare, if thou hast the understanding. Who hath laid the measures thereof, if thou knowest? Or who hath stretched the line upon it? Whereupon are the foundations thereof fastened? Or who laid the cornerstone thereof? When the morning stars sang together, and all the sons of God shouted for joy?"

The earth became alive. We defined life as a force to which the universe revealed itself. This revelation is accomplished through a universal communications system. Nature is the sending apparatus. The built-in instruments or organs of life are the receiving apparati. The medium is through energy forces traveling on waves. Life in various stages of sensitivity responds to the message by means of sensation. The more perfected instruments are enabled to receive and perceive wider manifestations of existing natural phenomena. They respond with more complex and diversified sensation. The response in sensation causes an increase in sensitivity of the receiving apparatus. In turn the improved receiving apparatus receives a higher level of knowledge from nature. It is this duality of action and reaction which explains the evolution of life from the simple to the complex. In effect it is the secondary creation gaining knowledge of the primary Creation.

With boundless exuberance and exhilarating joy, life filled the earth. With freedom of movement life explored the surface of the earth, beneath the earth, and in the air. Living creatures explored the seas from the depths to the surface. They crawled, walked, ran, flew, and swam. They explored deserts, mountains, and lush forests. They lived in light and darkness, in extreme cold and heat. The motivation was not the pursuit of food or for survival. Could the quest for survival or food explain why life left the familiar comforts, the protection of the sea filled with bountiful food in order to explore the unknown dry land? How many fish became extinct in the attempt to live in air equipped only with water-breathing organs. What was this magnetic pull which caused sea life to face incredible danger while in the process of developing air-breathing lungs? It could only be the desire to explore and experience wider and newer sensations on dry land which they apprehended with their senses.

At first they lingered but a moment on a beach; and their senses discovered new sensations. The visits to the beaches became more frequent and lasted just a little longer until they walked, crawled, or hopped away from the sea, never to return. Why would creatures leave the safety of solid earth in a lush forest in order to seek survival in the new and extremely dangerous form of movement in flight. They had to come back to earth to seek food while in flight—then why did they leave the source of food in the first place and travel through an atmosphere empty of food? For survival? They were seeking new sensations, new experiences, to witness for the first time new creations. They sought the experience of living.

How could such a fantasy as life exist? How can particles of matter see, taste, hear, smell, and touch? How can matter free itself from magnetic and gravitational forces and move—of its own volition? How could matter reproduce, gain the knowledge of producing—not only material forms, but even more amazing, they could reproduce an experience of pleasure or danger that occurred a million years before, through instinct. Who wouldn't want to survive in this miracle of creation? To see, even for another moment, light, shapes, forms, colors. To smell once more a hitherto unknown fragrance. To hear song, harmony, and chattering of life. To touch soft earth, the texture of vegetation. Why wouldn't the first law become the preservation of life? Not to survive for the sake of surviving, but to live—even courting danger, in order to pursue and capture a little more of Creation.

It is true that life is not all joy, fragrance, harmony, and pleasing texture. Life is also regression, pain, and agony. It is also degeneration, corruption, even extinction. There is decay and putrefaction, the terrifying sound of thunder, earthquakes, and tidal waves. Textures are often hard, sharp, gritty, and otherwise disagreeable. Our eyes see not only beauty but ugliness.

We are aware of the existence of negative forces of energy associated with degeneration. Physicists have discovered that the universe not only creates but also loses energy. Biologists are familiar with the process of degeneration in life energy. Philosophers and psychologists know these forces as the death wish and the tendency to destruction. Theologies know them as the forces of light and darkness. The Bible calls them simply good and evil. The basis of literature and art is the eternal struggle of the negative and positive forces, and they are called by many names. They are present in each person and seen in daily experience.

There are two reasons why we do not examine thoroughly these negative forces. One is that they have been thoroughly examined by professionals and experts. The literature of evil simply engulfs our present environment until the line between good and evil has almost been obliterated. Men now pretend they no longer know or recognize good from evil. Lawyers quote the Bible to prove the innocence of Fanny Hill. Once we knew. The positive forces of spiritual energy are barely flickering, and the declared aim is to snuff out this light and remain in the security of darkness. This will eliminate pain, agony, conflict, conscience, struggle, and man will be at peace. They are describing death, the death of the spirit. This is another onslaught on humanity to bring man down to the level of beasts.

We are not objective. We strongly favor the positive forces of energy and give them all the strength of body and soul we can muster. The negative forces are getting sufficient objective support. The potential destructive forces of energy existing in stockpiles of atomic weapons pose a threat of physical extinction. Geneticists are preparing to manipulate genetic forces of energy, hoping for biological survival. Darwinists and Freudians have removed man from his spiritual energy forces, and philosophers of despair have removed meaning and purpose from man's life. This poses a threat to his spiritual existence. Even theologians are preparing to dismantle man's last stronghold by removing man from his Creator. These forces do not need more assistance.

Cockroaches have survived on this planet for more than a hundred million years. How long will man survive? Arise, ye prophets, and answer. You can predict the movements of heavenly bodies and detect events spanning time periods of millions of light years. You can perceive and understand the march of evolution in terms of millions of years. You possess technical instruments—fabulous computers of which the prophets of old never dreamed. You are the creators of man's civilization and are preparing to dominate the entire universe. Surely you can make one more prediction. How long will man survive? You must be objective. Provided there is disarmament. Provided there is no further proliferation of atomic weapons. Provided there is an Atlantic Union or world government. Provided a Hitler or Stalin does not gain control of these weapons. Provided there is no accident of a human finger touching a mechanical button. Since you believe the entire universe was created by chance, why wouldn't humanity be destroyed by the same process. What do you say? Loosen the tongue from the roof of your mouth and speak. A hundred years, a thousand, or is it a million? Since we are mere biological creatures, different only in degree from animal life, we are inferior to a cockroach. The cockroach did better.

We will remind man of another prophecy—prophecy not hedged by provisions—except one. He came to the conclusion that men will prevail, and he pointed out the road and directions without hedging.

"And it shall come to pass in the end of days,
That the mountain of the Lord's
House shall be established as the
Top of the mountains,
And it shall be exalted above the hills;
  And all nations shall flow unto it.

And many peoples shall come, and say:
Come, and let us go up to the
Mountain of the Lord,
And to the house of the God of Jacob;
And he will teach us of his ways,
And we will walk in his paths:
For out of Zion shall go forth the law,
And the word of the Lord from Jerusalem.
And he shall judge between the nations,
And shall decide for many peoples
And they shall beat their swords into plowshares,
And their spears into pruninghooks:
Nation shall not lift up sword against nation,
Neither shall they learn war any more." (Micah 4:1-3.)

And Created Man In His Own Image

As in the creation of matter, vegetation, and zoological life, the creation of man means the primary creation. His potential was created in the form of potential forces associated with spirit. Man's materialization as a spiritual moral being is now, at present, in the process of evolution. His position on the spiritual ladder of evolution is approximately that of the appearance of a one-celled organism on the ladder of zoological life. Whether he ever will reach the potential which he possesses, or a particular level of his potential, or whether he will fail in the struggle depends entirely on his choice, his will, determination and wisdon.

Man's road is not that of chance or blind, effortless mutation. We do not know of any achievement of man that was reached in the manner described by evolutionists. Let us look at our own record, now—not a billion years ago.

A person is born with the potential of composing, playing, or singing music. Another is gifted with literary potential, still others learn athletic competition, professional careers, the many scientific disciplines; political, military, economic, or financial careers. In every case how does he reach his potential? by tremendous and sometimes superhuman effort. By education, work, practice, and most of all, discipline. In every case he must learn the laws of his chosen career, and abide by these revealed laws. he cannot deviate or he will degenerate to a quack physician, a shyster lawyer, a corrupt politician, an embezzler, or what we generally call a phony. Where are these mechanistic and chance occurrences—mutations? Or will you state that man is a freak, not part of nature? All investigations cry aloud the evident fact of continuity in evolution—never freakish development. Darwin's works are the textbook of documented proof of this fact. We quarrel only with the evaluation or value judgments of evolutionists, not their facts. Mutations are electrical impulses—after the event. They chart the progress or degeneration of a living creature in accordance with ascent or descent of life. they do not cause these events any more than a cardiogram causes heart failure. At the point of creation man was not yet materialized as a spiritual creature, even if his material form already walked upright, even if he already made tools, even if he possessed the proper shape of forehead and jaw. The creation meant that the plan, the concept, was completed.

"The lord God formed man of the dust of the

ground; and breathed into his nostrils the breath of life; and man became a living soul."

The breath of life is what we identify as energy forces associated with spirit or soul. At this point man was driven out of the Garden of Eden because he was no longer a zoological species. As a moral species he was no longer permitted to be tempted by animal instincts. The door was shut forever. Man was on his own and had to make his own effort to climb the ladder of spiritual evolution. There was and is no return for him. He faces either success on higher levels of life or death in the effort to force open the gates of paradise in order to return to the lusty pleasures of animal instinct. If man succeeds in reaching his potential, only then can he claim to be made in His image. The breath of life which man received only gives him the possibility of achieving his potential—a possibility denied to any other living creature.

As we begin to examine man, it will be simpler to test and prove many theories because we are living witnesses. We can deny or refute them in the language of reason and intellect. We can understand and accept conclusions more easily if they parallel our living experiences. We don't have to go back billions of years or reach out to eternity. We are prepared to face this most rigid test: the test of here and now—the test of facing man's stupendous store of knowledge.

The real difficulty lies in semantics. We must begin to use terminology which will mean different things to many men. Concepts of these terms have already been formed, and our lines of communication might become blurred and may even be severed. This is quite an obstacle. We must ask the help of those who read this and will patiently try to understand the definition in our context. It will be difficult for both of us, but it will be worth the effort.

We have discussed spirit and spiritual energy. What is spirit? It can mean spiritualism, seances, disembodied apparitions—for the superstitious or mystic. It can mean abstract or supernatural manifestations to the poet, or soul to the theologian. It can mean mind or spirited activity to the scientists. In our context we mean this: a spiritual force is capable of responding to a moral environment. The action and reaction, or duality between kinetic and potential energy results in work. Work produces matter. Matter is the end product of these energy forces which we measure, observe, use, and recognize. In this area we state that the forces of energy associated with matter are confronted with "the environment of matter." What else can matter be confronted with in our total environment but the environment of matter? Thus the "inherited" or created forces of energy confront this environment of explosions, implosions, radiation, cosmic rays, earthquakes, fire, water, etc. It was within this confrontation that matter was formed in innumerable varieties and evolved from the simple to more complex forms according to physical laws.

Zoological life also responds to and acts through the medium of energy forces associated with matter. It must obey physical laws which apply to all material forms. But they possess additional forces of energy associated with life. Here too, it is the action of kinetic energy upon potential energy which results in work. This work produces living activity. We call these life energy forces by different names. We identify the duality of sperm and ovum which produce cells. Cells are the potential force. They contain within their nucleus the forces of energy associated with life, which now confront the environment of nature. The inherited forces of energy act and react with the environment of nature, resulting in work which produces all varieties and species of life in accordance with the original potential existing in the primary creation. Thus zoological life can only confront matter and nature; it knows no other environment.

Man possesses forces of energy associated with matter; he confronts his material environment and obeys the laws of physics. Man also possesses the forces of energy associated with life, and confronts his natural environment; but in this area he is less law-abiding. This quasi-lawlessness results in his premature biological disease, degeneration, and death. But man discovers nothing in his material and natural environment which can understand, reflect, reason, know good from evil, is moral or immoral, speaks, creates civilizations, composes music, engages in art and literature. These are the end products of the work produced by his energy forces associated with spirit when these energy forces confronted and responded to the moral environment. No other form of life on earth is aware of any moral environment. Man began his evolution or his secondary creation, not as a tool maker, not as an upright animal. He began his evolution on his knees—in prayer, in worship, in response to his confrontation with the spiritual universe. In this area of life man is most lawless, and this is his danger.

Is this supernatural? It is as supernatural as the environment of civilization is to zoological life. We would call this supra-natural, or that environment which dominates all matter, all life—man himself and the entire universe.

In this movement or evolution from matter to spirit we note that in each stage of evolution the more complex forms begin to show tendencies toward the next step in evolution. They are harbingers of events to come. Thus the more complex forms of matter begin to display rudimentary sensations of life. If one looks for changes of form, he sees continuity by small, almost imperceptible changes. When the most complex forms of matter are placed beside the lowest forms of organic compounds, they are almost indistinguishable. But suddenly one displays living activity and the other does not. The difference is that one possesses a rudimentary potential force of energy associated with life whereas the other does not. Since energy forces are nonmaterial things and nonspatial, they can only be detected by their actions—by their work and by the end products.

In the evolution of plants to zoological life, the same process is repeated. The higher forms of vegetation begin to display tendencies of zoological life. Plants begin to move. They climb, creep, and attach themselves to moving objects. They also display the beginnings of digestive processes, replenishing their energy from other than earth and sun sources.

If one were to trace the evolution of zoological life, the same process of continuity is noted. The higher forms of zoological life display tendencies of spiritual or human existence. They exhibit rudimentary knowledge of communication, shelter, intellect, and tool making. The differences in form between simians and man are minor. The enormous difference in kind between man and animal is that man possesses the potential forces of spiritual energy; the animal does not. To study and gain knowledge of evolutionary processes, one must pay far more attention to energy forces.

Energy forces associated with matter are discernible as power and motion. We know their source; we know their characteristics. We convert these energy forces of matter to electricity, which powers our entire industrial civilization. We also know how the energy forces associated with life are regenerated. They are referred to as food: nutrition and vitamins. We measure them in terms of calories. We can convert them, add or subtract and change these forces at will. We also know their source in the earth and sun. A skeptic may ask: Where and how can we recognize and prove the reality of these spiritual forces of energy? As long as they remain in the area of poetry, philosophy, arts, and theology, we have no quarrel with the concept of spiritual energy. But when an attempt is made to define them as the third type of energy in evolution we have the right to ask these questions.

Now we truly face a hurdle in semantics. We submit that faith is the regenerative food of the spiritual forces of energy. We do not, in our context, define faith as confidence, trust, or any form of religious belief. We define faith as one of the forces of energy associated with spirit. Faith is energy because faith generates tremendous power—far more power than is generated by the industrial complex, far more power than is consumed as food by animal life. We do not define faith as power for good. It can be used as power for construction or destruction, as power for good or as power for evil. Isn't this also true of power generated by atomic fission or fusion? We use the term power in its most utilitarian and scientific context.

Power as a quality which has the ability to act upon a person or thing, the capacity to produce some effect, vigor, putting things in motion. Apply any rigorous definition of power and apply it to faith, and the conclusion is clear: faith is that power which regenerates the spirit.

Ask a physician to trace the materialization of this power in their experience with disease. Ask the soldier to trace effects of this power on the outcome of battles. Ask political movements or ideologies to trace their progress as the direct force or power of faith in their leadership—nation or ism. Ask those engaged in the most rigorous creative efforts in the sciences to trace the presence of the power of faith as the most important source of energy. The same power of faith is also present in inquisitions, in wars, and in the most evil acts perpetrated by man.

Faith itself is neither good nor evil. The need for biological regeneration is met when the appetite is satisfied. The requirement of faith to regenerate spiritual energy has no apparent limitation; its potential seems infinite. The power of this energy force can be changed or converted by man in accordance with his choice. It can be measured, accumulated, and stored. It can diminish or expand.

Its effects in the materialization of end products can be observed, seen, and tested. The potential power contained by faith is so enormous that it dwarfs the energy forces of matter. Compared to this power, the power of the sun's energy is a mere candlelight.

Proof: man, who possesses only a tiny fraction of this power which he received from "The Spiritual Sun," dominates life and nature on earth. The power of faith at its source in the spiritual universe dominates the universe. By every possible application of rigid scientific testing, the power of faith feeding the spirit is real. While we expend great sums of money, time, and effort to control, harness, and direct the vast store of energy associated with matter, we allow the forces of spiritual energy to roam with lawless abandon. Men should worry less about the damage from hurricanes, earthquakes, and tidal waves, and be more concerned with the force that can be loosed by the powers of faith.

How is this force of energy communicated? We can transmit energy forces of matter through the medium of wires or cables. The life energy forces are transmitted through the sun rays and converted into food. What is the transmission apparatus of this spiritual force of energy? Forces of energy associated with matter are activated when these forces are confronted with the environment of the material universe. The forces of energy associated with life are activated when they are confronted with the universe of life or what we call nature. The forces of spiritual energy are activated only when confronted with the environment of the spiritual universe. We received these messages and apprehend these communications through the medium of thought. Then thought converts these messages so that they may be digested by the spiritual organs of reason, understanding, logic, and wisdom. Man then responds through the spiritual sensations of love, hate, hope, inspiration, despair, dreams, intuition, vision, and prophecy. The end products are measured by the quality of good and evil. Only man has this capacity.

The spiritual forces of energy are subject to precise natural moral laws. These laws exist and operate whether or not we discover or recognize them. The laws of physics existed and were in operation prior to their discovery by science. The same is true of biological natural laws.

The decisive contribution of knowledge is that man could then adapt these laws to his own welfare and survival. This knowledge rejected the dark areas of magic, superstition, witch doctors, alchemy, and astrology. When men succeed in capturing knowledge by discovering his own natural moral laws, he will slough off the dark areas of his behavior. To discover these laws he must first recognize his unique spiritual environment. To discover his spiritual environment in knowledge he must begin by acknowledging the reality of the Creator—in knowledge. Without this knowledge there is only the darkness of superstition, fancy, and illusion. We can with effort know everything which is revealed to us in the environment of matter, life, and spirit.

"The secret things belong unto the Lord our God: but those things which are revealed belong unto us and to our children for ever, that we may do all the words of his law." (Deuteronomy 29:29.)

We began our search by frequent applications to man's own created civilization. We now continue to test our hypothesis in the most familiar and well—charted process of man's own natural conception, his growth from infancy and childhood to maturity. Since man is presently the third and highest form of life, he should display within his own natural creation many similarities to the whole creation. We have discovered the laws of physics on earth. We have not yet visited another planet, but no one doubts that the same laws of physics apply universally. The insignificant small model of the Tower of Pisa became the first working model to explore the motion of falling bodies. This is the method that should be used, by testing here on earth, by observing small-scale reactions, we can hope to deduce universal application of these discovered principles. Our laboratory turns to the conception of man.

The beginning is the fertilization of ovum. We now observe the action and reaction of two forces of energy associated with life: duality. The potential of mature and fully developed man already exists in these microscopic particles of matter containing all three forces of energy: matter, life, spirit. The energy forces of matter begin to produce the embryo. The embryo at an early stage is similar to particles of organic compounds of matter. As these forces of energy constructed what we call the embryo they were activated, guided, and directed by the life energy forces to produce the embryo. They cannot deviate from their directed course. They could be halted or changed only through the application of external forces. At this stage the life processes work toward the utmost protection from external environment. Soon the fetus begins to display rudimentary tendencies of the infant. It is heralding the birth of life.

Plant life is tied by its umbilical cord to earth. In the same manner the embryo is tied to its mother and receives its energy from that source. In its later stages the fetus displays characteristics of life; it begins movement, a sign of zoological life. The embryo undergoes a metamorphoses from early forms of zoological life, changing until it reaches its mature form. During the embryonic period it is still protected by the environment of its mother's womb, but it also begins to face danger. It can be affected by various changes of its host. It is not yet independent. The state of health of its mother will directly affect its guided growth. It can be starved if the mother hungers. It can suffer and die of disease affecting the mother. In short, its growth is influenced and activated by the environment of the womb.

The fetus is completed. This was no chance occurrence; mutations had no influence on its growth. Nor was it mechanistic unless we use the term in its proper sense—the mechanization or reproduction of a created original model in accordance with concept, design, and purpose. Even in this sense the growth of the embryo is not mechanistic, because it can be diverted, altered, retarded, and even halted by the activity of its environment. It is now ready to face a new environment. The fetus emerges from the womb, the unbilical cord is severed, and the infant now faces its external environment. It is frightened and responds with a cry. There is a difference in kind. The infant can now be well fed although the mother may starve.

The infant may be healthy even if the mother is not. It has achieved freedom. It is now an individual with a rudimentary display of independent action to its new environment.

Let us pause a moment for a review. Is it sensible to state that the original microscopic particles of spermatozoa were no different in kind, only in degree, from the mature man? Or by comparing embryo, infant, and grown man we see only a difference in degree? We know what will happen in continuity. We know that the original particles will not halt their evolution until we see the mature man, because the original particles already contained the potential of the mature man, because the plan, design, and concept called for the completion of a finished product. It was never intended that the particles should halt their evolution prior to the creation of the embryo. Or that the embryo would halt prior to the birth of the infant. Or that the infant would stop growing until adulthood. Or that man would halt his evolution prior to the appearance of the spiritual creature, the moral species.

With the completion of the primary creation the purpose and end product was already determined toward the completion of the moral species, spiritual man. At each stage there was a difference in kind. At each stage the advanced form displayed rudimentary properties belonging to the next. The continuity is observable and factual because this was the process of creating the universe with spiritual man as the end product. Man in his present stage displays rudimentary properties of the future appearance of the spiritual being—the moral species. At each point of change where a transformation in kind occurs, life achieves greater freedom but faces increasing danger. The only safe road is obedience to natural laws.

These natural laws guide life on the principle of freedom under law. This requires discipline and responsibility, without which freedom diminishes and life becomes extinct.

Man possesses the greatest amount of choice and free will of any other form of life. He is therefore at the most dangerous point of existence. He has not yet reached the safe plateau of the moral species and he has not moved far enough away from his animal past. But he can choose. He can no longer hide behind his rationalizations. He cannot deny that he possesses the great gift of knowledge. He cannot deny that he knows good from evil. Neither appeal to fate or predestination will help. He must choose his fate and reach his destiny or choose extinction.

"I call heaven and earth to record this day against you, that I have set before you life and death, blessing and the cursing: therefore choose life, that both thou and the seed may live." (Deuteronomy 30:19.)

We return to the child. Let us follow the course of evolution of the nonmaterial rather than discuss changes in physical form. We avoid this avenue of search, because the changes in form, from matter to human life, have been thoroughly examined by science and we can add nothing new. Although we are examining the evolution of man from conception to maturity, this is considered to be the model of evolution as a process.

The child responds to his environment by means of

his organs of sense. He cries, smiles, plays, and begins to reach, for he wants to grasp the identity of his surroundings. These responses are at first associated entirely with physical comfort. Consciousness is limited to biological needs. We see many resemblances between babies and infant animals. However, the child soon exhibits human characteristics which imperceptibly begin to differ from those of the animal infant. Oral sounds begin to articulate speech, indicating that he has begun to grasp the concept of language. Neither education nor environment explain why a young ape raised side by side with a human infant soon falls far behind in development. The child displays ever more complex responses and will continue to develop mature human tendencies.

Two children born of the same parents, raised in the same environment, may exhibit different aptitudes, behavior, and talents. They may differ in degree of dexterity and intellectual ability. Such differences cannot be explained by heredity, by genes and chromosomes alone. The differences between baby animals and baby humans, the differences between children in their aptitudes, talents and all nonphysical or nonmaterial characteristics, can be explained, defined, observed, or experienced by the qualitative evolution of consciousness. This consciousness is inherited and transmitted through natural and observable nonmaterial processes, which parallel the physical hereditary patterns insofar as both reproduce acquired experiences. In animal life the acquired consciousness becomes instinct, because evolution has ended with zoological life. In man we note a dual pattern. Since his biological evolution has ended, the physical reproduction is entirely mechanistic or instinctual. Since he is still at the stage of spiritual evolution, his nonmaterial heritage of consciousness continues to change in his own lifetime, either through progress or degeneration.

Scientists and educators do not deny that vast differences exist in the spiritual sense between one individual and another, between families, tribes, ethnic groups, and nations. They attribute these differences mainly to education and environment.

Environment is a term which means everything and nothing. Everything we are exposed to is called environment. However, one must be "conscious" of his environment. It is consciousness that develops, progresses, degenerates, grows, and is changed in the natural process of evolution.

Pigeons have inhabited St. Marks Square for centuries, and aside from becoming lazy and fat there is no evidence that these pigeons have changed so that they build altars in their nests or appreciate architecture and sculpture.

Thoreau sought a peaceful natural environment in order to contemplate and develop his philosophy of nature. Animals which inhabited the very same area for millennia have never changed their nonmaterial characteristics or instincts. A snake is still a snake, as is a spider, bird, or fish. They were "conscious" only of their biological needs and their habits changed when it became necessary to adapt to their biological environment. Nothing else, because they were not "conscious" of anything else.

Education used in its all-inclusive meaning *is* the transmission medium of spiritual heredity. This process is far more potent than physical heredity. There may be one heir or a million heirs who may inherit certain spiritual characteristics of one strong spiritual force through the means of spiritual instruments of communication. However, the process is not mechanical or depersonalized. A given amount of education transmitted to a class of a hundred students does not result in a quantitative predictable aggregate of understanding, knowledge, and perception. This process depends entirely on two personal—human and natural—factors. Once again: duality. It depends on the "quality" of the receiving agent, the pupil. Apart from the laboratory work, let the same teacher with the same knowledge, using the same text, lecture the same students by means of radio or records, and a significant and vital element of the educational process will fail. To be most effective the teacher must be present "in person." By being present in person, his personality, his "magnetism," even elements of "hypnosis" become important. What is communicated by this method is not only the material sound and text, but the abstract of meaning and understanding. It is literally an electric force process. It is the spiritual energy force which acts as the invisible spark which illumines and ignites the process of spiritual heredity through education. This element is what distinguishes the "quality" of one teacher from another, though both possess equal knowledge and both use the same text. Any student will testify to the truth of this observation.

When a teacher or tutor possessed of high quality not only of knowledge, but of personality and magnetism, teaches a student, the result has often been the development of some of the greatest figures in history who shaped our civilization. The larger the class, the more this magnetism is diluted and ultimately brought to a point of ineffectiveness. Great spiritual personalities possessing an immense concentration of spiritual energy force can effectively transmit spiritual heredity to large numbers of people. It is interesting to note that the Bible, which gives so much importance to genealogy in Genesis, practically ignores genealogy in the time of Moses. The progeny of Moses have almost no place in the narrative. Instead, the vast, all-powerful spiritual force of energy of Moses is transmitted to the children of Israel. Probably this is the reason why the Israelites remained in the wilderness for forty years. The new generation was thus able to receive from Moses in person the great spiritual heritage which has endured for centuries. This fact is impressive evidence of the existence of Moses as a living, breathing, historical figure of immense spiritual power.

Though visual and auditory mechanical devices play a peripheral role in the process of education, it is the teacher in person who is the foundation of this evolutionary process of the spiritual hereditary pattern. Man possesses the most sophisticated instruments of mechanical communication, yet he does not consider for a moment an attempt to automate education completely. Why not? It would solve the problem of burdensome taxes, high tuitions, and could spread education en masse from cradle to grave. What is it that a professor does that cannot be recorded on tape or visualized on television or printed in books? Every possible question debate engaged in between pupil and teacher can be anticipated statistically through laws of probability. Technically it is far simpler to automate education than to produce automobile parts. Certainly the amazing powers of computers can be developed for this purpose. Yet the demand for teachers grows by leaps and is insatiable. The demand for reducing the size of classes is insistent. The demand for more "personalized" teaching persists. The quality of a college or school is measured by this "personalized" criterion and the results justify these demands. Despite fanciful claims, "learning" mechanically while asleep or through the use of drugs is a mental aberration.

So much for the sending apparatus. How about the receiving apparatus—the students? But for spiritual heredity or consciousness, each student would enter the classroom as a blank sheet of paper waiting to absorb education. Each student would be equal in the ability to understand. I.Q.'s would be unnecessary and entrance exams would be superfluous. Each student would emerge at graduation with the same grades, and his achievements in life would be predictable and mechanical. We need not waste space to challenge these silly assumptions. Everyone knows the opposite is true. The so-called potential, the so-called inherent intelligence, the so-called aptitudes, talents, and abilities are manifestations of the quality of consciousness, naturally transmitted at birth and developed through evolutionary methods. This is obvious not only in college but in the cradle. Children of the same parents, raised in the same environment, exhibit vast differences in spiritual characteristics from the cradle to adulthood. This is why animals can be bred scientifically and why the attempts to "breed" certain types of humans have always failed. The only way one can breed human types is through persistent social pressures of uniformity. It must eliminate choice, diversity, creativity, and arrest the development of consciousness. This can be partially achieved only in a closed society tyrannized by philosophical or material chains or both.

Formal education is not the whole pattern of natural spiritual heredity in evolution. It may not be the most important in nontechnological areas. Education as the process of spiritual heredity begins with birth. The communication system is not exclusively in the form of vocal or audible language. It can be the language of love. It can be acts of kindness or brutality which are experienced by consciousness. Of course parents and close relatives play a dominant role in the development of spiritual heredity patterns, but not exclusively. Associates, playmates, friends, nurses, guardians all contribute to this two-way process. The transmission is always from person to person. Some of the world's greatest geniuses were raised in poverty and in a slum environment. Criminals, tyrants, degenerates, and morons were often raised in an environment of affluence and luxury. This too may be observed and proved statistically.

Though consciousness is the memory of our past nonmaterial experiences, the measure of man is his quality of moral consciousness, found nowhere in zoological life. Our child does not reach maturity only because he can walk upright or because he has grown to a specific height or because he achieves physical dexterity. Every civilization measures the maturity of man by his inherited quality of moral consciousness. This is recognized in our legal code, it is recognized by all humanity.

We call the destructive actions of children mischievous, naughty, or bad. But we do not hold a child responsible until he reaches moral maturity. He is then held responsible for his actions. He knows good and evil. He is no longer an animal. He may choose evil and risk punishment. Or he may have inherited a perverted or low quality of moral consciousness and we offer psychiatric treatment. He may have inherited such a low quality of moral consciousness that he must be sent to an institution in the interest of society. The point is that we act on this principle of inherited moral consciousness whether our attempted cures and disciplinary actions are right or wrong. They cannot be right unless we recognize the fundamental cause. We must search into the workings of moral consciousness.

It is tragic and a seeming injustice to be born with a retarded moral consciousness. It is an equal injustice to be born poor or to be devoid of talent, gifts of harmony or art or intellectual capabilities. In our own civilization, in a free society, we take measures which afford every child an opportunity to advance, even slightly, by his own efforts. He may attain wealth in many ways. He is afforded an opportunity to become aware of music, art, and science through education. Except in extreme cases every person who lives his life in a free society can add a little to his inheritance and thus improve the quality of his descendants, and his community, his nation, and indeed all of humanity. Why do we expect less in the development of the most vital force of all humanity—moral consciousness? If men know this and yet choose evil ways and thus diminish the quality of their hereditary material, why do they complain about injustice? Man is the product of what he has done and will become the product of what he does now. Most men know they can bequeath their material wealth to their descendants. Would they do less if they knew they can also bequeath the gift of humanity to their descendants? What kind of world do we have? What kind of world will we have? No political treaties or organizations or philosophy will provide an answer. Nor will wealth or education or military force. We will have the kind of world that we make now—only by one method: the acquisition of increased quality of moral consciousness. This is fundamental in man's evolution, everything else is temporary and illusory.

Can we use the measure of success in any vocation as a yardstick of evolutionary progress? A man may become a fine physician and successful, but he can develop into Dr. Mengele who practiced abominable experiments on men, women, and children in Nazi concentration camps, or he can become a Dr. Schweitzer. He can achieve political mastery and become a Hitler or a Winston Churchill. He can achieve literary skill and produce pornography cloaked in the style of the classics, or he can produce *Paradise Lost* or The Psalms. What is the measure of evolution? Or is there no measure. Humanity has long ago decided that there is a difference between one doctor and another or one political leader and another. The measure is always in the quality of moral consciousness.

Even the rise and fall of civilizations can be measured with the same yardstick. The difference in the development and growth of North America and South America can be succinctly stated as the difference between men seeking liberty and men seeking gold. Everything else is a consequence of the initial drives of the Founding Fathers. Men point with pride to the abolition of slavery as a far greater achievement than the size of skyscrapers. We are not trying to sermonize. We are not even suggesting that men should change their behavior. We are trying to gain knowledge of processes. Then men may choose.

A physician may prove that smoking cigarettes may cause cancer of the lungs. Men will continue to smoke but they must not bewail their unjust fate, having made their choice. We are trying to trace natural phenomena which can be subjected to research, to knowledge. The most basic instinct of biological life is hunger. Life depends on the satisfaction of this basic requirement for survival. The energy produced by food can be converted to many activities. The basic instinct in the moral species is moral consciousness. It is energized by the food of faith. The resulting energy may be used for good or evil. This spiritual energy is utilized by man to develop his civilization. His literature is based mainly on the conflict of love and hate, freedom and slavery, and cowardice, nobility and venality, virtue and corruption, good and evil. This is also the theme of his music, his art, his law, his politics and his humanistic sciences. Moral consciousness is not a material thing, but is everything.

This knowledge is vital to man. If he knows the cause of many ills besetting humanity, he has enough intelligence to seek a cure to arrest degeneration and to protect himself from its dangers. Mawkish sentimental outpourings of sympathy alone will not cure or heal.

It is tragic when a person becomes addicted to dope. It is even more tragic when children born of dope addicts inherit its lethal effects. But the problem of curing or arresting this disease is our challenge. In the meantime society must protect itself from the destructive, irresponsible actions of dope addicts. Our sympathy and concern must be extended to any innocent victims of this disease. Why should an innocent person be penalized for the tragedy of another? With contagious diseases, we legally and medically isolate the victims to protect the health of the community.

If we investigate, we may find that an appreciable number of Germans no longer inherit a significant quality of moral consciousness. While the children of Nazis are not responsible for the actions of their parents, they may well be an even greater danger to humanity because they may be bereft of moral consciousness. They are victims of a disease. Humanity must recognize their affliction. If they recognize this they must take steps to cure, arrest the disease, or to isolate them for the protection of society. The symptoms will not be difficult to discern if we look for them. The first stage will be degeneration of moral behavior. This will be followed by inability to know good from evil. The inhuman actions of their fathers will be measured by success or failure to complete the extermination program or failure to win the war. Hitler is dead, but he left a powerful legacy which may still be prevalent among certain numbers of Germans. We have avoided value judgments or predictions. We break our discipline for the sake of man's survival. There will be no atomic war by any nation except one instigated and ignited by those Germans who have not inherited any significant moral consciousness.

The quality of awareness is a sensitive instrument for detecting danger even if we are not yet conscious of the danger in knowledge. Despite the fact that Germany possesses no atomic weapons, that its war machine is under the discipline of NATO, that Russia has massive and overwhelming superiority in atomic weapons matched only by the United States, Russia does not fear that the United States will ignite a nuclear war. Russia still fears Germany. Not only Russia, but all of Germany's neighbors are apprehensive of a danger they cannot define.

This does not imply any suggestion for mass punishment or eternal revenge or forgiveness. On the contrary, by pointing out the area of disease it is still possible to halt its spread and even to begin a gradual rehabilitation. The methods used in war criminal trials or sermonizing or education would not be effective. It must be an attempt of an unprecedented applied spiritual therapy. It will have to be administered with a great deal of courage and discipline. The first step is diagnosis. The second step is revealing to the victims the extent of their spiritual disease. They must know that their choice is between a thousand-year Reich or an eternal ascent in evolution. Since they know that a cockroach will never dominate as long as higher animals survive, they must also know that, unless they resume their march on the rungs of life through the evolution of moral consciousness, they will become the future cockroaches of human society. The change will not and cannot be dramatic and sudden. The results will not be achieved by complete demobilization or destruction of their material machinery. It must be directed by humans possessing moral consciousness—and there are enough Germans to begin this process.

It must become the effort of individual Germans. It must be disciplined and fought by Germans, for Germans. It must be positive in form. The results may be slow and even imperceptible, improvement or degeneration will be noted in small and insignificant evidence of individual moral behavior. It may be necessary for the growing children to be faced with a very stern environment of moral behavior. The entire civilized world and especially its European neighbors must encourage and respond to this effort. They could do no better than to mount a program of moral regeneration of their own. Cynicism, hypocrisy, and deceit will not achieve the goal. As Abraham Lincoln said, "You may fool some of the people some of the time." But you will never fool nature and nature's Creator at any time. This is a battle for keeps. The stakes are enormous. Do we have the courage to face this problem squarely or shall we continue to rationalize in the confused terminology of would-be creators?

Let us once more return to our man: He is now mature. We will offer no advice or deliver lectures. He will be informed in a thousand ways how to enter college, how to discipline himself through study and achieve high grades. He will be guided by innumerable I.Q. and aptitude tests to help him choose his vocation. Many institutions will guarantee him peace of mind and happiness. Commercial and financial corporations will vie for his services and guarantee him decent pay, fine homes, entertainment and all sorts of fringe benefits. Should he fail to live up to his potential, he will be able to count on unemployment insurance, welfare benefits, and social security. We have nothing to offer that is better. We state once again, for emphasis, we are not searching for material phenomena. Our quest is for the monmaterial, the "nothing" which you will discover is really everything.

My dear mature man standing on the threshold of your own life. Are you really assured of everything? Who and what will ease your loneliness in this vast universe? Who and what will ease your gnawing hunger for spiritual food or faith? Who and what will answer the real questions of your soul, questions which you are diffident even to vocalize, but they persist, why? What is the meaning, the purpose, the goal? Why did I arrive and where am I going?

With all your empirical learning, these questions will persist. You will try to shut out these troublesome promptings in various ways. If you are lucky you will throw yourself into intensive, unrelenting drives for success and be relieved now and then by diversions. You will feed your ego for sustenance, but the whispering of doubt will remain. Or you will deliberately try to drive out your inherited soul and long for the contentment and pleasures of animal life.

You simply cannot carry the burden of human existence without fulfillment. But neither can you reach the level of animal life no matter how you try. Animals can satisfy anf fulfill their inherited instinct. Their appetites have been conditioned and their potential is limited. You will find that your sensual or biological appetites cannot be fulfilled. If you are unlucky you will turn to alcohol or drugs to anaesthetize your insistent longings. But periods of sobriety will come. Each moment will bring an eternity of pain, of damnation. You will require more and longer periods of intoxication to ease your agony. You will embrace and yearn for death; but will death end the torments? Clinically, the particles of matter we call genes seem to transmit your torments to your descendants. You are now confronted with the relentless laws of nature. All your artifices of civilization will be of no help. You will simply have to face your problems—as a man, not as an animal. You will have to feed your moral consciousness in order to find fulfillment.

One cannot rationalize about the need for food. One doesn't argue whether eating is rewarding or desirable or necessary. We have long ago accepted food as a natural requirement. We shall have to learn to accept the vital need of food to satisfy our spiritual needs. We may even find it pleasant and delectable. It may even be far more exhilarating to our senses than alcohol or drugs. It may even become more satisfying than catering to our ego. One does not preclude the other. One complements the other. All our successes will have meaning and purpose. We will be exhilarated by natural and lasting perceptions of moral consciousness—not by bypassing such perception through the use of L S D or other drugs, but by and through a natural process, under natural moral laws.

What are moral laws? What are the standards? My dear mature man, do not take refuge in sophistry or cynically fabricated pseudo-science. Be brave enough to look into your own moral consciousness. Will you say you don't know good from evil? Will you tell yourself that you cannot differentiate lewdness and perversion from purity and wholesome natural desires? Will you say that you cannot discern a difference between barbarism and civilization. If there is the slightest response in your soul that there is a difference, then you still possess the priceless ingredient of humanity. You may, if you wish, choose evil, but you will know an evil act. There is hope that when you or your descendants pay the penalty of nature, you will resume the ascent of life in evolution. But if you no longer recognize good from evil, then we as humans bid you farewell. Because you will become the species of cockroach in the hierarchy of human evolution. Remember just one thing: this was your choice. Don't bewail and cry out against divine injustice. You have your opportunity; you can take it or leave it. You are a mature man and must accept responsibility.

What are these natural moral laws and how do we discover them? If you begin to ask these questions you have already decided to climb the ladder of life. There is not pat and final answer. It is the quest for these natural moral laws that is the responsibility of all humanity. It is not only your problem—it is ours. To begin with, we were not created in this generation. All of us possess a family genealogy and a national genealogy. We did not spring suddenly out of the primeval forest. Through research, can you identify the basic phenomena that were chiefly responsible for the rise and survival of civilizations? Can you see only a difference in industrial production between so-called developed and underdeveloped peoples, or is there a nonmaterial moral difference? Can you predict the rise or fall of your own family or nation based only on material accomplishments, or are there far more important signs of moral behavior which we must observe?

Study cause and effect. Be severely practical. Above all, do not rationalize; use the method of science wherever it might lead, as long as it is proven in knowledge. Experiment and demand tests of these nonmaterial moral phenomena. These tests, unlike other experiments, must be made only on human beings. But contrary to abominable physical experimentation, the tests and experiments of developing moral consciousness and discovering natural moral laws present no possible danger to humanity. Can you predict any harmful side effects from living a more moral existence even by present ill-defined standards?

Be on guard against sudden and dramatic change. This is not a sign of evolution. It is a signal of fanaticism which may burn brightly but dangerously only for a little while. The road of evolution is signaled by slow and almost imperceptible changes. We must reckon changes in centuries, not days. The hearts of men will be lifted in hope—the hope that someday men will reach their potential as a moral species. It will be a sudden event, heralded by tendencies toward the spiritual species. But it can be a goal here and now, a promise for the future, and your life will have meaning and purpose. This is something. You will recognize the products by their universality. If it is a natural moral law it will apply to all men. You will recognize it by a new category of man. Not measured by race, religion, or color, or even by technical know-how.

The new categories will be measured by the degree of moral consciousness possessed by any individual man or groups of men. When this becomes a mark of distinction, all men will join in the struggle for the ascent of life. Since it is in the nature of man to struggle and accept challenges of superiority, the battlefield and the weapons may change. It may turn into a real race to reach for the stars, with or without space ships. This will be evolution, not revolution. The institutions of man will evolve. His arts, his science, his political and economic institutions will serve as vehicles for the one victory which is eternal. His atomic stockpile will not be disarmed by treaty. But men will be disarmed of suspicion, corruption, greed for power, and they will simply leave these monstrosities to rust and become archeological wonders.

Is this Utopia? There is one difference, and a vital one, between this utopian dream and all others. This is no plan or new system devised by the hands or mind of man. We shall either discover its existence in natural phenomena or it isn't there. We can return to corruption and evil at any time. We can always destroy ourselves. We need only a truce on a universal scale for a limited period of time in order that we may expend some effort in discovering these natural moral laws.

One must never forget that regardless of political

systems or religious or color divisions, all are human and they might just respond as humans. Will this solve border problems or problems of power domination? We don't know. Have they ever been solved by recourse to the machinery built by man? The problems may well remain for a hundred or a thousand years, but it may no longer matter very much. Men will be bored by the worn out power plays and take up a new and more exhilarating struggle for life itself. The only ones who can lose are the tinhorn, loud-mouthed would-be destroyers who will be laughed out of their jobs. Incidentally, the first task if men wish to start this experiment is to demand silence on the part of these pretenders. We must have silence if we hope to hear the voice of the real Creator.

Let us now return to our mature man, who is now an old man. Well, old-timer, you have gone the entire journey and you are now where you began. Or are you? During your journey, events occurred. Evolution never stands still. Did you fall back a notch, advance a fraction, or were you simply indifferent to life? What difference does it make to you, since your life will soon end? This is the big question, immortality! It is another question that cannot be answered. It takes its place beside the questions of the essence of energy, the beginnings of the universe, the transformation of matter to living activity, and the transformation of zoological to spiritual life. There can only be one answer for immortality, for there is only one answer to the other transcendental questions. You must look to the Creator for answers to all of them. Surprisingly, we can find a clue in our own created civilization.

Why do you think our creators of civilizations enshrine their deeds in literature, history, and monuments? They vehemently deny natural immortality but they carefully make sure of their own immortality. Isn't this a result of spiritual awareness? Do you know of any animals that prepare their immortality? Where did these men get this concept? They conceived it as they did all spiritual or human concepts—as a discovery of natural phenomena, as an imitation of nature, or as a consequence of their natural evolution. But examine carefully the method men use in preparing immortality for their created civilization. They do not offer or promise material rewards or sensual pleasures in idyllic gardens. They only recount and immortalize the *deeds* of men who traveled in the orbit of life. That is all—but that is enough. Who would ask for anything more than to have his worthy and glorious deeds enshrined in the book of life? Who would see it—who would care?

It is the essence of all creators to be jealous of their creations. To create a universe from an immaterial thing to a moral species is an inconceivable accomplishment. Such a glorious achievement cannot culminate in a void. It is not natural. Not in man's created civilization nor in the Creation.

"And God saw every thing that he had made, and, behold, it was very good." (Genesis 1:31.)

II

The Thesis and Darwinism

We choose as our battleground, literally and figuratively, the problem of race relations in the United States or the Negro revolt. It is fair to state that this problem presents a worthy challenge to any theory. The consequences resulting from success or failure are enormous. So much has already been written on certain basic causes that repetition will shed no new light. Nevertheless one must not submit to easy assumptions. There is a measure of truth in pointing an accusing finger at ghettos, illiteracy, unemployment, and prejudice as very important factors as a cause of revolt. These factors, both political and economic, must and should be corrected.

It is also true that these are not the only factors inflaming the heart and soul of the Negro. They may not even be the *most important;* because it is also a fact that among the ranks of the rebels, and perhaps leading the rebellion, are the educated, the skilled, and the employed, the well-fed, well-clothed, and well-housed. If prejudice was the most important factor, then why did the rebellion erupt at its most furious in areas where prejudice was relatively mild and rapidly diminishing, as in Detroit and New Haven? There may be another and perhaps a more decisive cause which can be apprehended and, if corrected, we may find a cure.

It is a historical coincidence that just about the time the emancipation of the American slave was being proclaimed, the Darwin theory was also proclaimed. In the wake of Darwin's shattering proclamation, there developed a consensus among the world's leading biologists and evolutionists that the Negro was just a little higher on the ladder of life than a chimpanzee and on the lowest rung in the hierarchy of the human species. This was taught in schools and printed in textbooks. Not only that, but the Darwinists gave the Negro no hope of escape. He could not rise through his own efforts because the "law" stated that acquired characteristics are not hereditary, and he was doomed to extinction by the "law" of natural selection. This period was followed by the "science" of eugenics. In its period, eugenics was as respectable as genetics is today. This "science" gave birth to pseudo-sciences of the "master race" with the Nordics at the top of the ladder. The "law" of the survival of the fittest gave a spurious but effective base for the practice of genocide on all "inferior" races.

Darwinists are properly ashamed of this period in the history of evolution and they have made corrections. In this process the basic postulates of Darwin's theory pertaining to man's evolution were thrown on the rubbish heap of discarded false theories. The sorrowful fact is that a truncated and twisted Darwinism is still the bible of the life sciences, and many disciplines are still tied to it.

The average Negro may not have read Darwin. He may not even know that it bears any relation to him; but he has felt its searing effects. He has seen its effects in the contemptuous eyes of those white men who have read Darwin, who endorsed eugenics. Even Dr. Schweitzer's compelling force for aiding the Negro was the feeling of compassion for children left behind and doomed in the race of evolution. The Negro's manhood was questioned. His consciousness was deeply scarred. He has been wounded in the most delicate area of a man's existence—his spirit.

Our thesis states a universal law, applicable to all men, regardless of race or nationality: That all men are created with an unlimited spiritual potential energy force enabling them to rise on the ladder of life through the development of consciousness, the highest and most important being moral consciousness. That this potential will reproduce in an hereditary pattern when it is exercised, regulated, and disciplined in response to an existing environment, guided by moral laws. That we recognize frankly and honestly that the low grade of various spiritual consciousness apparent in large numbers of Negroes is due to their exposure to an environment of the jungle for many centuries, and the American Negro bore the additional burden of being exposed to a cruel, dehumanizing, and degrading environment of a slave society. By recognizing these factors and bringing them out in the open for examination, we may find the real underlying cause and apply the cure.

In accordance with the thesis, the rise of the Negro people will depend on two things: (1) They must be given the opportunity of confronting the best possible environment to permit their development of consciousness, (2) Like all people in history who have risen on the ladder of life, the Negro must respond to this environment by his own effort. No one will push him up the ladder of life. He will have to make it on his own. This is the law of nature and it is universal—it applies to all men. The Negro can claim no exemption unless he wants to remain an object of compassion.

While the Negro can and should continue to fight for his just economic and political rights through the instruments of his own organizational forms, the development of moral environment is not a Negro problem; it is a human problem. And here it is an American problem. In this mixed (color) organizational form there will be no patronizing atmosphere. It will be composed of men who are determined to create a moral environment in these United States, not only so that the Negro may climb the ladder of life but also for the sake of the white man. This would be a real partnership of equals. Here again, the Negro cannot claim exemption. A moral environment cannot be erected on prejudice and hate. This too is universal and cannot be altered by any group. The results in terms of diminishing criminal violence on the streets of America will very quickly be apparent. Thus every citizen will benefit and be thankful. If the Negro will detect in the eyes of the white man a rejection of Darwinism in its popularly accepted meaning, if he detects a look in the eye of the white man which says: You are equal in potential; you are a free and complete human—in time you will rise ever higher on the ladder of life—from that point on, revolution will end and evolution will begin.

Ah, you say, you are whipping a dead horse. These race theories you speak of have been completely rejected. Not quite, my dear Darwinists. Have we ever heard a confession of guilt from your learned journals? The original theories played havoc with the lives of millions of men and altered the destiny of humanity. You claim to have rejected the theories. Then how do you account for your reverence toward the author? How is it that Darwin's evolution is still your bible? Are you a science or a cult? The popular notions of Darwin's theory have never caught up with your sophisticated changes. Scientists, no less than other men, must redeem themselves through full confessions in order to purge themselves from this enormous guilt. Instead, Darwinists have spawned a new monster—far more dangerous than eugenics. This new science of genetics, when it is experimenting on humans and when such experimentation is based on Darwinism, is dangerous not only for Negroes but the whole human race.

The new genetics based on the proposition that "ideal" men can be reproduced through the manipulation of genetic material has been too widely advertised to require repetition here. Other sciences enforce strict rules in terms of definition, and certainly in curbing fanciful imagination from entering the portals of science. There is a place for imagination: it is called science-fiction. Although science-fiction is usually based on scientific speculative thought, it is not permitted to profane the pure sciences so painstakingly arrived at through research and supervised testing. Little wonder that humanity respects scientists and the institutions of science.

This is not true of those geneticists who fill the radio, television, popular magazines, and popular books with untested, unproved wild speculations which are even too fanciful to be classed as science-fiction. Their continued abuse of scientific privilege will in time undermine the layman's confidence in all science. Academic and scientific freedom carries with it the responsibility of exercising these freedoms. Unchecked, irresponsible statements by any category of the scientific and academic establishment may result in legislative controls of the present freedoms. This would be a pity. But the other sciences will have to bestir and involve themselves much more deeply than at present if they wish to avoid disaster.

Let us examine a few specific examples. At a recent meeting of the Academy of Sciences held in Washington, D.C., the world-famous and esteemed geneticist Dr. Theodosius Dobzhansky does not deny the possibility of manipulating human genetic material to produce an "ideal man." His worry is: "One must decide what sort of man is the ideal to be striven for." The late Professor Herman Joseph Muller, a Nobel prize-winning geneticist from the University of Indiana, made it plain for everyone to understand. At a symposium held at the University of Chicago to commemorate the centennial of the first publication of Darwin's *Origin of Species* Professor Muller states: "In the service of this 'new morality,' foster pregnancy, made possible by the techniques of artificial insemination, would be welcomed. This trend would be greatly promoted as techniques and facilities are improved and accepted that allow the transfer of both male and female germ cells or potential germ cells; their accumulation and maintenance in frozen or in multiplying condition; and their rational testing, selection, and manipulation. Thus," he said, "children can be adopted not merely after birth but even, as it were, before fertilization. This will provide the opportunity of bearing a child resulting from the union, under the microscope, of reproductive cells one or both of which may have been derived from persons who exemplified the ideals of the foster parents.

"These reproductive cells, both male and female," he said, would "preferably be derived from persons long deceased." For this purpose, banks of deep-frozen reproductive cells would be maintained, and also multiplying cultures in them. This procedure would make the most precious genetic heritage of all humanity—the genetic endowments of the Einsteins, Beethovens, da Vincis, Shakespeares, Lincolns of each generation "available for nurturing into childhood and adulthood."

I am not so foolhardy as to enter into a debate with such outstanding intellects on a subject which I know only from what I have read in responsible scientific books. I would like to pose some questions to those geneticists who affirm, or at least do not deny, the above statements.

We have been taught by biologists that acquired characteristics are not hereditary, that they do not become a part of genetic material. Then what are the geneticists trying to reproduce? The long, lanky frame of Lincoln with his deep sunken eyes? Or are they trying to immortalize the mole on his face? How can you produce the "ideal" man by reactivating the deep-frozen reproductive cells of Lincoln? What made him "ideal" was his great love of humanity, his great intellect, his courage, his wisdom, and above all, his highly developed moral consciousness. In accordance with your theory all of these attributes are acquired characteristics and would not be found in the reproductive cells of Lincoln.

We assume your answer will be that the "ideal" man undergoes a "cultural evolution" and that you consider the Lincolns, Beethovens, da Vincis, and Shakespeares as outstanding products of this cultural evolution which you wish to preserve. As usual, Darwinists are rather ambiguous in their formulations. We still do not know whether their research has proved that the acquired characteristics of cultural evolution are hereditary. Evidently this is what they imply, otherwise their projects of developing the "ideal" man simply fall apart.

But this is not the end of this Lincoln story. You stated that "children can be adopted not merely after birth, but even, as it were, before fertilization." This could lead to some interesting situations. It is logical to assume that if Lincoln's reproductive cells were now available, some good Republican family would adopt this child born from the fertilization of Lincoln's genetic material. This good Republican family might possibly live in the deep South confronting a segregationist environment. Our reborn Lincoln might grow up to become a racist. What would we do with our Lincoln Memorial? We don't need your "new morality." Our Lincoln whom you so much admire was born, raised, nurtured and grew via the "old morality." We know what our "old morality" produced and we hope to do better. Who knows what your "new morality" will produce? Maybe the things which will crawl out of your laboratories may have the biological structure of a man, but may lack moral consciousness, sans love, sans faith, sans soul.

We present our thesis as a challenge to Darwinists and to the genetics based on Darwinism. The thesis suggests one universal law of evolution applicable to all living creatures. It explains the differences between animal life and man. It shows how acquired nonbiological characteristics are transmitted in an orderly and lawful pattern both for human and for zoological life. It indicates a direction which men must take in order to produce the ideal man. It also describes what ideal is to be striven for.

If cultural characteristics are hereditary through a process of learning instead of sexual means, then it is not present in genetic material. Then what is the purpose of freezing reproductive cells? How does one freeze a nonmaterial instinct in animal life, or courage, intellect or moral consciousness in humans? If cultural evolution is a universal natural law, then why do aboriginal children achieve scholastic supremacy in Australian state schools and no attempt is made, nor will one ever be made, to send simians to school?

When they state that "cultural characteristics are hereditary through a process of learning," isn't this another term for acquired characteristics? Learning must be a process of acquiring. Then we would have two contradictory laws of evolution. One would state that "acquired characteristics are not hereditary," but "acquired cultural characteristics are hereditary." If only they would free themselves from Darwinism, the answer comes through loud and clear: All acquired characteristics are hereditary as long as the species is still evolving in life.

When each species reaches its maximum potential it can no longer change its hereditary material, biological or cultural, except minor variations produced by external or artificial means. Therefore animal life and humans are no longer in a process of biological evolution; and only man is in a process of what they call "cultural evolution." Therefore acquired characteristics were always hereditary under natural laws of evolution.

There cannot be a law of evolution for life which is no longer in the process of evolving. Only life "in" the process of evolving can be described in a natural and universal state of evolution.

When creatures halt or are halted in their evolution, their present characteristics, behavior, growth, and development are of no value in research of the process of evolution, because they might have grown, behaved, developed in an entirely different way when they were still evolving and under the influence and direction of laws of evolution. What can stone or metal tell us about evolution except as a possible pattern of continuity?

All zoological life has come to the end of the road of what scientists describe as biological and cultural evolution. (Our thesis describes both of these forms as one process.) The eel cannot learn through natural means how to breed in other seas, nor can it ever learn by natural means the direction to the Red Sea. When men "teach" animals whether to perform, amuse or serve them, these "lessons" are not hereditary. Men have saddled horses since the dawn of history, yet every new generation must be broken to the saddle. Mules never seem to learn.

The farther back we go in evolution the more deeply frozen is their "culture" and biology. Ants and bees must have sometime "learned" how to perform in the most highly ordered and most sophisticated society known on earth below the level of man. Even a sluggish man was once advised to learn industrious qualities from an ant. Not only have they ended their evolution, but it occurred so long ago that man cannot even teach, train, or make friends with them. The simians, which ended their journey in evolution more recently, are far more amenable to processes of teaching and learning through man's artificial processes. Yet, if you took a bicycle-riding chimpanzee from Broadway, released him in a jungle populated by members of his own species, he would forget all about *Variety,* the show-business paper. He would doff his trousers, strip to his natural state, climb a tree, eat a banana, and scratch himself.

Man was once in a biological evolution and his "cultural evolution" was limited to "learning" to take care of and improve conditions for his physical welfare, like any other creature. He, too, developed some biological instincts which remained with him, and very basic ones will remain with him forever. While in this stage of evolution, all his acquired characteristics, both biological and cultural, found their way into his hereditary material. It was a slow process. It was painful. It was difficult and arduous work—it was a great effort spanning millions of years—but man finally made it. He stood on his two legs and now his face could look upward to the skies, to the heavens. When the Lord spoke, only man could look up and answer. When he received his spiritual or moral endowment, man ended his biological evolution. Therefore man can no longer inherit acquired biological characteristics, but can and does inherit acquired "cultural characteristics." No other animal life does either. Man is the only creature on earth still under evolutionary laws.

This is not poetic fancy. This is science and can be put to the test. Scientists have identified biological ancestors of man going back to two million years. They also trace rather important physical changes during this long period. Posture, shape of forehead, jaw, and other physical changes are noted. Consider this: Neanderthal man was the immediate predecessor of historic man by approximately 40,000 years. The skull of Neanderthal man was on the average some 150 cc. larger than the skulls of our most famous geniuses. His other physical endowments which we have noted at the dawn of history were superb. It seems that man had reached the maximum of his biological potential and his biological evolution ended. Now about his "cultural evolution"? If he possessed the skull and brain capacity and his superb physical endowments, and if these are the only qualifications, then what was man doing for two million years? There is no evidence of slow, gradual, almost imperceptible cultural progress which is the evidence of an evolutionary process. At the dawn of history some six to eight thousand years ago, man leapt from caves to palaces and pyramids. He almost immediately began to write, which proved he could also speak a language. Though the language symbols were at first crude, a shorthand kind of art form, yet the messages recorded were already highly imaginative thoughts.

Note what man accomplished in the past six thousand years. Can you imagine what he will do in the next two million years? We are well aware of many theories. The development of agriculture, fire, the wheel, and many other involved speculations. What we do know and need not speculate is that when man began his own spiritual, moral evolution as evidenced by the historic appearance of one altar of worship, from that point on, man went his way alone. No animal marched by his side and kept step with his forward momentum. And he did it, and ironically, despite some regression of his physical endowments. Man advances with smaller skull; all of his senses are deteriorating and are far inferior to animal life. Whether he be a hunchback, short, tall, fat, lean, sick or healthy, deaf, mute or blind, we will show you individuals who have advanced man's evolution despite those physical handicaps.

It is interesting to note that the Torah describes men of huge stature and others living over nine hundred years. At the same time, the Torah describes the beginnings of a new form of life and the great difficulty of this life in making headway against such powerful physical forces. The moral species will make its appearance on earth when the spiritual-moral forces within man finally conquer and dominate his inherited biological forces. It will be a lawful, a scientific method which can and will be noted. Many tendencies toward this coming of the moral species will appear from time to time in the form of great moral and spiritual individuals. This contradicts statements that the "nature of man" is unchangeable. Such men are saying that man has reached the end of his cultural evolution. This seems to be the road his is now taking when he persists in looking down to animal life, instead of up to the heavens. Little wonder he cannot hear the "voice of the Lord."

The emergence of the moral species will not be the result of chance occurrence or mutation. It will be the result of a tremendous purposeful effort. It will be agonizing and painful. Evolutionary changes are always slow and barely perceptible. At some point in time which we cannot know, the moral species will emerge triumphant and the cry of Eureka will be joined by the cry of Hallelujah.

The Darwinists are not without critics within the scientific establishment. The following quotations are taken from the Philadelphia *Evening Bulletin* of April 17, 1966.

> *Scientists Assault Darwin's Theory*
> *but Fail to Agree on Another One*

The birds, the bees, the fish in the sea, the moons of Jupiter and the fruit fly all have something in common. The behavior of each was cited as were many more things—to support arguments as a blue ribbon group of scientists spent 42 hours here attacking the theory of evolution as advanced by

Charles Robert Darwin in 1859.

The meeting was held at the Wistar Institute, 36th and Spruce Sts., beginning Sunday evening and ending yesterday afternoon.

Some 35 of the world's most renowned scientists argued to the point that they shed coats and loosened ties as the conference room warmed and the air turned blue with smoke.

When they had finished, Darwin's theory had been badly battered, but the scientists failed to come up with a better one. "I think we have at least defined the argument between the biologists and the mathematicians," said Dr. C. H. Waddington, of the Institute of Animal Genetics in Edinburgh, Scotland, as he summarized the conference, "and I think we biologists have profited, though I'm not sure the mathematicians have." Dr. George Wald, Professor of Biology at Harvard University, was chief advocate of the long-standing argument that part of evolution is cultural, so that it cannot be entirely biological.

He cited the eels that always go to the Sargasso Sea to breed, that being something they have "learned" to do. The same thing can happen in humans, Dr. Wald argued, as when a childless woman teaches school or engages in social work, or cares for a nephew or niece—"she is contributing to evolution without reproducing."

A major question of the conference was whether mathematicians could produce, now that they have computers capable of handling very large numbers, a theory that would be better than Darwin's.

Dr. Marcel Schutzenberger, Professor of Mathematics at the University of Paris, France, who also holds a doctorate in medicine, was the most outspoken of the several mathematicians present. He described the immensity of the problem and said no computer that man can now build can encompass all the data necessary to describe all the different things seen in nature, let alone fit them into an orderly pattern.

By agreement at the beginning, there was no discussion of the influence of God or any form of Supreme Being.

III

The Thesis And Torah (Pentateuch)

We limit ourselves to the Torah rather than the Bible, because it is not our intention to enter the discipline of Biblical scholarship or get into religious controversy. We are not qualified for either task. We suggest the following ground rules taken from these two quotations.

(1) "The secret things belong unto the Lord our God: but those things which are revealed to us belong unto us and to our children for ever." (Deuteronomy 29:29.) (2) Scientific symposium: "By agreement at the beginning, there was no discussion of the influence of God or any form of Supreme being."

The Torah acknowledges that the things that are revealed to scientists are the property of man, and the scientists seem to agree that the secret things belong to the Lord. This is a good beginning and will make our task easier.

Scientific discovery of natural laws are basically a nonmaterial creative process culminating in revelation. It is conducted primarily through communication.

There is archaeology. When an archaeological site is discovered, scientists begin a dialogue with the mute evidence of past history. They subject the discovered materials to many searching tests. This is their method of asking questions. When the mute materials finally give up their secrets, the result is revelation. It is an arduous and laborious process requiring great skill, knowledge, and specific training.

Bedouins found the Dead Sea Scrolls accidentally and sold them for a few dollars. When the highly skilled archaeologists completed their tests, the scrolls were revealed as priceless. Historians try to translate ancient language into modern language. This is a more direct form of communication between the past and present. It is still very difficult and only the most highly skilled men with great knowledge are able to conduct this dialogue. Not only must they break the code; they must also translate. They must search for idioms and esoteric meanings of a different time, a different place, and a different environment. The historian brings to bear all of his magnificent faculties before he receives a reply. When the answer comes, it is revelation.

The life sciences face far more formidable obstacles when they conduct their dialogue. Test and test again, endless and repetitive experimentation. Constant observation of the specific and the general. Direct and statistical information is required. A host of technologists are employed in this monumental task. Grudgingly and slowly, biological life answers the questions. But not clearly. Each day, each year, refinements and corrections are necessary when the knowledge is applied, and sometimes they do not conform to predictions.

When a Pasteur, a Dr. Fleming, or a Dr. Salk receives an answer, it is revelation. Accidents have nothing to do with this process. Dr. Fleming had to be there in person when the now famous accident of a spilled test tube occurred. Had it happened while the charwoman was present, we would not possess penicillin. She would have quickly cleaned up the mess.

The discovery of fire was not accidental. Natural causes have been responsible for fires since the time that combustible gases and vegetation appeared on earth. Zoological life and even men observed such fires for millennia, but they did not discover fire. What is this searing hot material which consumes things before our eyes? They wondered. Can it be used to consume things at our discretion? Can we control it so that it will keep us warm without consuming us? They conducted a dialogue with fire, and when the answer came it was revelation.

The apple that fell from the tree had nothing to do with Newton's discovery of the theory of gravitation. Newton possessed the mind of a genius. He was highly trained in the knowledge of mathematics and astronomy. He spent sleepless nights and long hours of the day observing the movements of bodies in space. Constantly and endlessly he put questions to the physical universe. He conducted an extremely difficult dialogue with this universe. With the force of prodigious energy, Newton finally received an answer. The physical universe revealed itself to him. Newton spent most of his time in his study. If he took a walk for relaxation on a beautiful spring day and rested under an apple tree, he was probably fast asleep when the apple fell.

It is not a coincidence that educators couple these rather superficial occurrences with sublime acts of creation. We must wonder whether these stories are planted for the purpose of proving that the progress of evolution is the result of chance occurrences or mutations instead of purposeful, orderly, lawful creative processes. When natural events are artificially interpreted to fit unproved theories we are in the area of fancy and mythology. It is a great privilege for any theory to be incorporated into science, but it must be forced to obey the very strict rules of scientific procedure.

Men also possess the faculty of imagination. They are gifted in the arts: painting, sculpture, music, poetry, and many forms of literature. They too conduct dialogues with the harmony and beauty of nature and they use their enormous gifts to magnify for us the things which are revealed to them. The exceptional ones border on prophecy. We know and appraise their efforts when their works appear, and we judge the worth of their prophetic insights. When the content stems mainly from imagination, we label the product fiction or abstract art or abstract music or science-fiction. We either enjoy them esthetically or we don't. If an imaginary product is inferior when put to the test of judgment, we do not accept the quality of its revelation. We grade it in various categories. When one tries to present an imaginary dialogue without any product which may be tested, we dismiss it as fancy and sometimes hallucination. Mythology is mainly a product as a scientific guide to ancient civilizations. No archaeologist looks for mythological sites. No biologist searches for a unicorn, centaur, or fire-eating dragon. Mythology is not based on law and proposes none. In short, it is never offered as a test in human experience. Of course, they may contain fragments of actuality, but these are very meager.

We can delay no longer. We must confront and try to explain revelation in the Torah. We shall try to thread our way very carefully and avoid stumbling over a hornet's nest of religious controversy and Biblical scholarship. It will be proof of a minor miracle if we succeed. As we stated in the thesis on Creation, a process may show similarities, yet display enormous differences. Still, similarities are important and perhaps decisive guides in determining universality. Science and the Torah, each can contribute to the fashioning of a basic instrument of research which could help both the scientists and Biblical scholars. As in the analysis of Creation, I stated that I do not know how this took place. I also declare that I do not know how the revelations in the Torah took place. We are trying to discover a process, not the *act* of Creation or revelation. One of the enormous differences is this: in science, man is the dominant being on earth, addressing himself to inferior creatures in nature. In the Torah it is the reverse. Man is the inferior creature, conducting a dialogue with God. As in the thesis, when we conceived of a primary and secondary creation, let us conceive the Torah as the primary revelation and subsequent revelations as secondary. With this concept let us try to illustrate this principle in our experience.

Suppose we characterize Einstein's theory of

relativity as a primary revelation of the physical universe. Let us suppose that a young student with little or no knowledge of mathematics or physics reads this revealed theory in a book. The student is intrigued with what he has read but cannot understand a word, even with the aid of a dictionary and a glossary of mathematical symbols. We can state that Einstein is dominant and the student is inferior.

The student wants to gain knowledge of the theory of relativity. He begins by studying higher mathematics and physics. He wants to communicate with Einstein, but before he can begin a dialogue he must learn the language. Whether the dialogue is conducted in a classroom or directly with Einstein is immaterial. The dominant figure, Einstein, cannot answer the student's questions if the receptive qualities are lacking. One cannot carry on a meaningful dialogue on philosophy or econmics with a child. The dialogue is always limited to the receiving capacity of the inferior partner to a dialogue. The student if intelligent is prepared to pay the price in learning the difficult language of mathematics and physics. As he progresses, the dialogue begins to reveal its meaning to the student. What was the change that took place in this process? The theory of relativity remained exactly the same; not a word or symbol had changed; nothing was added or subtracted from the original text. The change took place on the part of the inferior partner of this dialogue. The student now begins to experience revelation of the secondary variety.

The primary revelation is Einstein's theory of relativity. But students all over the world and in many generations will experience secondary revelations in varying degrees, always limited to their own quality of receptiveness and understanding of the terms. Any student may apply this knowledge which he received from Einstein and test whether the predictions contained in the theory are accurate. But he must follow the laws stated in the original theory, otherwise the tests are meaningless.

How does one test supernatural events—since man can only test natural events? Let us try to test things which are revealed to us and permit the other events described to remain secrets belonging to the Lord. But the entire work is suspect as a valid source of scientific knowledge for those who consider this sacred Book as mythological in character. This evaluation in no way belittles or denies its unique character in the history of man as the foundation of monotheism and its supreme ethical, moral, and inspirational messages.

Is the Torah Mythology?

Let us put it to some tests. Ask the archaeologist. While they do not waste time even to seek mythological sites, every archaeologist consults the Torah for clues and direction. Some even study Hebrew in order to guide them in their excavations and the interpretation of their finds. Have archaeologists found corroborative scientifically acceptable evidence? They have—in profusion! Is there a scholar of ancient history who does not study and consult the Torah for clues to ancient civilizations? Have they discovered scientifically acceptable evidence of the accuracy of the Torah? They have—in profusion! Is the Torah based on law which can be tested in experience? The Torah is so much a source of law that it is called "The Scroll of the Law." The word itself is translated as "Law." Consider "The Decalague." We know that the Commandments have been largely ignored in actual experience; but what is their claim to predictability? No law, moral or scientific, can be tested for predictability by violating its rules. The test of predictability is possible only by obedience. Have any predictions made in the Torah proved accurate? Many have, but not all. Let us be patient—and forewarned. Just as science eliminates fiction and fancy from its revelations, so the Torah rejects any revelations based on superstition, clairvoyance, and all forms of the black arts. There are severe penalties for infraction of these rules.

But what about mythological tales, legends, and folk stories which have been discovered in the most ancient civilizations and in almost every part of the globe? Many of these tales bear striking resemblance to the Torah and a few are almost identical. Isn't this conclusive evidence of the mythological nature of the Torah? Evidence submitted by past civilizations cannot be conclusive. By necessity, they must be circumstantial in character. If we consult a living civilization, consult living men and contemporary culture, we might arrive at a new and different perspective—far more reliable. We, in our time, know who composed our immortal musical classics. Beethoven, Bach, Brahms are not figures of mythology. We also find that snatches of melody have been taken from these classics and converted into countless popular songs. They are published, sung, and played in every culture and in every language in every part of the globe.

How do we judge which is an original product of revelation and which are fictional copies? Archaeologists five thousand years hence may argue that this is proof that Beethoven, Bach, and Brahms are the products of mythology. We know better. Apply the same test when examining a sublime revelation in the Torah and the brief snatches which appear in mythology which have no beginning, no middle, and no final movement.

But we overlook a very important point. Religion is based on dogma. We don't want to face any more trials of Galileo. One must not confuse the Torah with the monotheistic religions based largely, but not equally, on the Torah. There are vast differences in interpretation and practical application. There are even more numerous divisions within the body of the three monotheistic religions. We reiterate, our investigation is confined to the Torah. There is nothing in the Torah which bars Galileo's laws of physics or any other proven laws of science.

We must take into account that Christianity is indebted to Aristotle for much of its philosophy. Artistotle, not the Torah, stated that the sun moved around the earth. It was Aristotle who "proved" by very involved mathematical calculations that the heavenly bodies were all designed as perfect circles. It was Aristotle who submitted a law of motion which described prime movers. Christianity reacted honorably and nobly to defend Aristotle, not to defend the Torah. Inexplicably, scientists and the entire community of intellectual thought revere Aristotle and summarily reject the Torah. There may be other valid reasons for this discrimination, but the Galileo episode is not one of them.

By this circuitous road we now come to our thesis. As much as we wanted to avoid this area of investigation, it is not possible to speak of the Creator and not carry on a dialogue with the Torah, the primary revelation. Admittedly, we entered an area which is most deeply shrouded in veils of mystery. Any suggestions or claim that we found the answer or that an answer was revealed to us would be a blatant fraud. We did detect one pinpoint of light breaking through the heavy mists. It consisted of one word—"work." Genesis describes the Creation in terms of "work." The Lord "worked," "He made," "He formed"—all are expressions of work. To further emphasize this prime principle, the Lord rested on the seventh day. This is not all. To further hammer this term into the consciousness of man, the Sabbath was incorporated into the Decalogue—forever. When I consulted scientific books for the definition of "work," they told me that it was entirely a process of energy forces—nonmaterial, nonspatial, and indefinable. From this description of "work" I also found that, to create man, it was not only necessary to form him, but that a new force of energy was employed: "And the Lord God formed man of the dust of the ground, and breathed into his nostrils the breath of life." (Genesis 2:7.) Thus the thesis was written. Whether this is a secondary revelation depends entirely on man's tests and evaluation.

One cannot discuss revelation and not refer to the Prophets. The Torah is the primary revelation beginning with man's origin and ending with prophecy. The Prophets take up this thread and their revelations unfold man's destiny. Thus the Torah is "one" complete symphony. The first movement begins with the universal origin of man. The second movement describes a specific nation that did not choose, but was chosen, to play out this cosmic drama. The props were all too real. Oceans of blood and tears. The screams of children are still reverberating throughout the universe. Courage was enacted in dungeons, the torture chambers, and concentration camps. The human soul was tested in "acts" of struggle and despair. They also revealed many and serious weaknesses which required painful corrections.

What kept them going was the knowledge of His love and waiting for the moment of ecstasy when He would make His presence known to them. One cannot endure for long an extremely precarious journey directed toward disappearing horizons of eternity. Then how did this people endure for millennia? They did not endure for millennia. They endured for six days and they rested on the seventh. With this cosmic rhythm they can endure forever.

The Prophets received their cue to enter the stage where this cosmic drama was being enacted. They had witnessed the drama unfold and they were horrified. They cried out in bitter protest. They refused to participate. Only when the Lord revealed to them man's destiny did they agree to perform their part in history. This was the third movement of this cosmic symphony; the first movement begins with universality and the third movement ends with universality.

Thus we have reached the limits of our potential. All further questions and explanations will have to be undertaken by qualified scholars.

IV

Knowledge and Belief

We must pause for a moment in order to more clearly define various terms which we use and to explain our unique approach to the quest for knowledge.

When the term science is used, the instant association is with confirmed knowledge. When the term "theological" is used, the instant mental association is with unconfirmed beliefs. These are difficulties of semantics. The fact is that a scientific theory is not yet knowledge and must remain in belief until verified. The fact is that a substantial part of theological thought has already been accepted by man as knowledge. This is particularly true in the area of morals and ethics. Any theological belief which can be verified becomes a part of man's knowledge and is universal.

The presentation of a belief or theory is accompanied by divided opinions and heated debates Men choose sides and champion their beliefs. This usually results in the organization of sects, creeds and isms. When beliefs are verified through scientific investigation and brought into the arena of knowledge, the result is harmony and universality. There are no debates now whether the earth is flat or round. There is no Einsteinism or Newtonism. There is Darwinism.

The scientific method is to introduce theories or beliefs with the still voice of reason. Scientists invite and welcome open debate and criticism. They are searching for knowledge. Often a scientist may present a theory and at a later stage criticize his own theory on the basis of new facts. For example, Wallace, who shared honors with Darwin on the theory of natural selection, wrote the following letter to Darwin:

> The mental requirements of the lowest savages such as the Australians or the Andaman Islanders, are very little above those of many animals... How, then, was an organ developed so far beyond the needs of its possessor? Natural selection could only have endowed the savage with a brain a little superior to that of an ape, whereas he actually possesses one but very little inferior to that of the average members of our learned societies.

This letter was met by stony silence and was never answered by Darwin on the advice of Huxley. Wallace was punished for his impudence by gradual isolation. But Darwinists found their voice very quickly in directing their passionate fury of ridicule and mockery on those who dared to disagree. They are still using the same tactics: silence on any provocative questioning of Darwinism and furious personal attacks on the author. These clashes were not between an established knowledge and a belief, but between one belief and another.

Life and Immortality

The kind of immortality which is defined as perpetual life without degeneration and death or the transmigration of souls, or a form of life after death can not be brought into the realm of knowledge. Such speculations must remain in the realm of beliefs.

We define immortality as a natural force of potential energy associated with life. As a natural force it is found in all life and made its appearance with the first manifestation of living activity. It is universal and therefore a proper subject of study for scientific investigation. We postulate that the act of reproduction was in response to the force of immortality. That the unification of cells into clusters, colonies and organisms was a cooperative effort of life motivated by increasing the probabilities of immortality through the survival of larger units, which were far better able to defend themselves against the possiblity of extinction. That the universal instinct of protecting the seed of life and caring for the offspring, even risking individual death in the process, stems from the force of immortality. It may also be the primary reason why members of different species do not mate and cannot fertilize life. The reproduction of a chicken does not serve the immortality instinct of a monkey and vice versa. The force of immortality antedates the instinct of sex because reproduction was performed in asexual forms of life.

In the social insect groups such as bees, the sovereign power was conferred on the queen bee, the material instrument of fertility serving the force of immortality. Darwinists have correctly identified fertility as the measure of fitness in evolution. But this definition applies only to animal life. Insects have probably become immortal. One may examine an ant now and compare the specimen with an ant a million years hence, and find no marked difference in their physical appearance or social activities. Geneticists are now trying to duplicate this feat for the benefit of humans; but living organisms who ate of the fruit of knowledge can no longer attain immortality. They possess a new and dominant force of spirit. They can only survive by forever reaching for expanding moral consciousness. If they fail, they will die.

But the basic force of immortality inherited from animal life continued to activate and influence the lives of men. The Pharaohs responded to this drive by building pyramids. Pagans and idol worshippers tried to infuse the illusion of life into inert matter. Stone, marble, gold and silver were symbols of immortality. Those who worshipped the sun, moon, stars and all objects in nature also responded to symbols of immortality. Pythagoras, the founder of Greek rational thought, embraced the doctrine of the transmigration of souls. The Greeks conferred immortality upon their mythological gods. The Roman Empire was powered by belief in the immortality of its Emperors. They could and did co-exist with conquered peoples who worshipped their Emperors, but could not abide competition from any other symbol of immortality. All kings and conquerors reached for immortality by perpetuating their fame and glory in history. They engaged their private historians as they engaged their private artists to build the equivalent of pyramids.

As any other natural universal force, immortality is neither good nor evil. This drive may explain the extraordinary burst of creativity of the Renaissance. The so called dark ages of Christianity which preceded the Renaissance were the incubating period which built up the powerful force of immortality. This period of the dark ages was saturated with speculations of heaven, hell and the after life. This was probably best expressed by Dante's *Divine Comedy*. When the explosion occurred, the creative energies of the artists and composers were inspired by and directed towards the eternal and the infinite. Men of wealth vied with each other to patronize the arts in order to grasp at immortality.

In the modern, rational 20 century, scientists try with mighty exertions to be pinned by the Nobel Prize of immortality. Captains of industry and finance willingly give up a part of their sovereign rights to stockholders and form corporations, a symbol of immortal life. Board rooms proudly display portraits of their founding fathers.

The spirit of man could no longer be served only by the force of immortality inherited from animal life. Man displayed a new and unique dimension which is not found in animal life. Men surrendered their lives for the survival of non-material, abstract ideals of justice, freedom, liberty and to expand their consciousness. Men left the comforts of civilized nations of Europe to pioneer in the dangerous undeveloped wilderness of America. The motive could not have been the instinct for physical survival. Their chance for physical survival was appreciably reduced by their pioneering. Men willingly faced danger in the exploration of new territories. Travelling in covered wagons was not conducive to physical survival. Men fought for their ideals on every battlefield of the world. The pioneers and warriors left their bones scattered in the wilderness and lonely deserts.

They lost their lives in the air and in caves. Martyrs of every age willingly surrendered their lives in response to a higher force. These men responded to the dominant spiritual force of their being. They fought and died for survival, but not for the animal force of immortality through physical reproduction. They fought for the survival of spirit, for freedom, liberty and to apprehend new horizons of creation through the evolution of moral consciousness. This is knowledge written in the blood of martyrs. Our technologies were not built on the foundation of the physical and material. Our technologies were built on the foundation of man's spirit. This is a difference in kind and not a difference in degree. Death caused by natural degeneration or accident is not a punishment under moral laws of nature. Man survives because the martyrs died. This kind of death is rewarded by developing higher forms of life through the evolution of the spirit.

Extinction and Death

The arrival of the atomic age demolished all of man's illusions about immortality. It is not decisive whether or when someone will push a button and extinguish all life on earth, because if this happens we will not have a problem. What is decisive is that all the artifices and certainties of survival have already been shattered. For the first time the earth and life on earth are mortal. His pyramids, the empires, the mighty nations, the stone idols—nature itself, the monuments, the immortal arts, the financial and industrial corporations all live under the threat of extinction. Extinction not only blots out the future of man but it also blots out his past. It not only means that man will not be, but that man never was. The life expectancy of man has been reduced from experience in eternity and infinity to the quantitative measurements of three score and ten.

The creators of our civilization taught men to ignore beliefs, hope, inspiration and to rely only on proven scientific knowledge. When humanity puts to them the questions of survival or extinction, our wise men fall back on beliefs and hopes. They believe that mutual deterrents will prevent doomsday. They hope that non-proliferation and disarmament treaties will prevent atomic war. They pray that an accident will not trigger the explosion of a hydrogen bomb. Even the most orthodox Darwinist will not try to comfort humanity by stating that if there remain but a few microbes on earth and a few species of fish in the sea, then evolution through random mutations guided by natural selection will again evolve into man in a billion years, give or take a hundred million. In a crisis, men will turn to Isaiah for comfort.

But man can not return to beliefs. The assurances of statesmen and the wordly wise do not comfort him because these statements are not based on knowledge.

Man has been conditioned to respect only knowledge. Strangely, the books of theology, which men ignore because they shed no light on technology, may be the only repository of information which may be tested through the scientific method and perhaps answer the question of survival or extinction. To mount such an effort, the discovery of the creation of life in a test tube may be set back for a century. We will just have to get along with present methods for another century. Space exploration may be set back for a century, but Mars and Venus will still be available for exploration a hundred years hence. The question we want answered is, will man still live on earth in a hundred years. It is simply a matter of priorities and will. If we still have the will to live, we will find the right priorities. The terminologies such as love, justice, good, evil, eternity, infinity, redemption, salvation, etc. will be very strange to men's ears. We will learn to get used to such terms, as we have learned to live with the strange sounds of DNA–RNA, Repressors, Messengers, Enzymes and the bewildering terms of psychologists, behaviorists and sociologists. We may even learn to like these old terms; they may even be a source of pleasure. They are certainly more inspiring and who among us can't use a little inspiration as we watch the dark clouds gathering which threaten to blot out our destiny? Every well organized research must have a goal which may be applied in experience. What are we searching for? We are searching for the source of the observable, measurable and experienced energies of matter, life, spirit, faith, immortality and evolution. We are searching for the eternal and infinite. When we apprehend the source through knowledge, it will become universal, the precious possession of every man on earth, now and forever. Is this a call for a universal religion or a theocracy? It is neither. These concepts are problems of semantics and must be clarified.

Theological institutions will remain as the jealous guardians of their accumulated treasures. The various religions in all their diversity will continue to serve their members who share a common belief. They will continue performing their rituals and singing their litanies which are unsurpassed for the experience of inspired beauty. They will continue to comfort man who will have to face mysteries of life which can never become knowledge. They will continue their superb scholarship in revealing, interpreting and clarifying religious thought. And this is our point of departure. When an article of belief or religious theory is examined through universally approved secular, scientific methods, and if such investigation results in its entrance into the realm of knowledge, such a belief is no longer the private property of any religious group. It now belongs to all men, forever. Then theologians and scientists will both drink from the common fountain of knowledge as they now drink from the same fountain of mathematics and physics. There is no longer a conflict as to whether the earth is flat or round. Neither trials, circuses nor passionate polemics solved this problem. It was solved by the still small voice of knowledge.

A theocracy is a government of mortal men who want to enforce moral law based on their beliefs. Such a form of government denies the right of man to seek knowledge through the apparatus on his own spiritual evolution. Theocrats erroneously believe that an institution can evolve higher forms of spiritual life through the process of evolution. But evolution beckons individual men and not an institution. It is the individual man who has a rendezvous with destiny. Institutions may die and men live. But if man dies, institutions can not live.

The functions of institutions are to supply men with the freedoms and environment which will enable them to rise on the ladder of life. The Declaration of Independence, which gave birth to the United States, meets these needs. It states that its principles are "derived from the laws of nature and nature's God." Though derived from natural moral law, the Constitution and the vast codes of law were arrived at through secular, scientific investigation and they are constantly being changed. The only document which can not be changed even through majority vote is the Declaration of Independence. If men wish to destroy this document, they will first have to destroy the United States. This Declaration of Independence is the sovereign power of the United States and this power is in turn derived from the Sovereignty of "nature's God."

The Universal Force of Sovereignty

A force of sovereignty can be proven through knowledge even if one does not know the sovereign. If you will travel to a strange country, you will not be met by the sovereign, but you will meet the sovereign forces which rule. It will be a self-evident fact. This is the method by which we can gain knowledge of The Creator.

A sovereign force reveals itself through rule of law, the ability to enforce the law through punishment and the possession of the ultimate force to which all of its component parts must submit.

Rule of Law.

We are all generally familiar with the existence of laws which rule the world of inert matter and mass. These are laws of physics. We are also familiar with biological laws which rule all forms of living activity. We postulate that man is also subject to the rule of moral law. We can detect some very sharp questioning: Morality is an abstract. There is no standard. Morals are an absolute etc. etc.

If you can ask these questions, you are educated. You do possess conscience. You have been raised in a family unit where you might have been exposed to definitions of good and evil, right and wrong. You did go to school and have a little knowledge of laws covering ethics which were derived from nature. You have some inkling of Biblical literature. Please don't play games of sophistry at this point of our history. It is not humorous, it is macabre. You know the difference between good and evil. You know the difference between right and wrong. You know the difference between the actions and behavior of a noble spirit and a knave. You know that men vary greatly in their attainment of moral consciousness. If you know, let us not waste time in interminable sophistry. If you don't know, then your soul is dead and there is no point in a debate. If you say that you do know the difference between good and evil and choose evil when such an action is not punishable by the laws of your society, this is quite different. There are punishments for such actions.

The Enforcement of Moral Law

The individual law breaker will continue to degenerate in life, poison his life material, depending on whether he breaks biological laws of life or moral laws of the spirit. If he breaks the biological laws he will shorten his life span. If he breaks moral laws he may be cast out completely from the stream of life and face oblivion. Dante's *Divine Comedy* was still the framework of life sensation. Oblivion experiences no further sensation though we can never be certain that oblivion may not be conscious of its nothingness. This is neither mysticism nor superstition though it is still speculation. Because we already know that our actions can and do affect our reproductive cells which can result in damage to our life material. We know that our characteristics and instincts will make their appearance in the future. This is knowledge, not belief.

How will you know this without memory and why should you care? Your hereditary material does have memory. As far as your personal memory is concerned, you don't know who you were, yet you suffer or enjoy the consequences in the present. This is the only life material you may ever possess. It would be an act of wisdom if you took care of this most precious possession.

The third test of sovereignty is the possession of the ultimate weapon. I think we can agree that the ultimate weapon is no fantasy, no belief, not just an expression of poetic fancy by inspired prophets. We can now see it. It is right over our heads. But we can still choose—we can choose life and good.

Summary

What is the purpose and goal of writing the book? Since we have discussed so many subjects, where is the evidence of unity of thought?

Our purpose was the examination of man himself. Not the examination of any of his parts nor the examination of the nature of his activities, nor did we search for the mysteries in Heaven. Our first obstacle was that of definition. No science will undertake serious study without the prerequisite of definition. Such a definition must apply only to man and must be identified as the property of all men.

We went to the physicists and asked how they defined matter. We were told that matter is made up of elementary particles which are bound together by the four different kinds of forces associated with potential energy. The biochemists identified the elementary particles of living matter but did not identify the potential energy forces which could account for living activity. All activity must be energized. We suggested that living activity is energized by potential energy forces associated with life; and since we observed the spiritual activity of man, we suggested that spiritual activity is energized by forces of energy associated with spirit.

Having stated this we had to identify at least one potential force of energy in living activity and spiritual activity. This led us into trying to define immortality as one of the potential forces of energy associated with life and to define faith as one of the potential forces of energy associated with spirit.

Having reached this point the problem then presented itself in terms of natural law. What are the natural laws which may be applied to spiritual activity? Thus we began to examine natural moral laws which regulate spiritual activity. From these definitions we arrived at the definition of man as a moral species. This was contrary to Darwinism.

I did not relish the task of joining battle with Darwinism. It is a comparatively simple task to challenge knowledge. One simply presents new facts which undergo scientific investigation and everyone submits to the decision. Historically, beliefs are far more difficult to challenge. How can one challenge mountains of documentation with nothing more than insights, even if interesting and inspired?

We now had to define revelation as the natural process for the acquisition of knowledge. If documentation is the prime factor for the acquisition of knowledge, then the rivers of data compiled by scientists, state departments, business and industry which now are fixed in microfilm, in the memory banks of computers, in text books and libraries would surely have solved all of man's problems.

Documentation is the technological instrument to check and test a theory first apprehended by revelation.

We then turned our attention to origin and destiny. What is the use of defining man unless we know his origin and destiny? Surprisingly, none of the life sciences including Darwinism shed any light on man's origin or destiny. There were vague allusions to missing links which have not yet been discovered. They pointed to evidence of fire, agriculture, art, artifacts and toolmaking. None of this evidence brought us any closer to the mystery of man's origin and destiny.

Torah is very specific on the subject of the origin and destiny of man. But science considered Torah as a collection of beliefs based on mythology. Therefore, we were forced to meet this challenge or abandon hope that secular scientific methods would ever be used to examine Genesis as a source of possible knowledge. The reader can appreciate what formidable obstacles such an attempt would face; but we could not abandon this project. The stakes were too high.

Since Genesis identifies God as Creator and the Sovereign of the universe, our task was to interpret the language used and to bring this into the arena of man's own experiences of his own created civilization. The self evident facts had to become evident to man on his own terms before he would accept them as facts. If we tried to avoid this avenue of search then all the other related theories would collapse like dominoes.

We entered the arena of political science when we undertook the examination of sovereignty. The prevailing theory that nature and natural forces are sovereign can easily be proven to be erroneous. We have discovered laws of physics and biological laws here on earth and we extend these findings on the level of universality. This is both proper and necessary. Its predictability has been proven accurate in space explorations.

Here on earth man subdues, adapts, harnesses, controls and utilizes nature and natural forces in accordance with his own will and desires. Nature does not prevail in exerting its pressures of selection upon man. It is man who exerts his pressures of selection upon nature. It is man who decides which objects in nature will live or die. Thus the sovereignty of nature can not be a universal law.

Is the sovereignty of man a universal law? If so, then man's exploration and conquest of space will establish him as the sovereign of the universe. Since the sovereign force of red communism was in the hands of Stalin, then it follows that a Stalin could be the sovereign ruler of the universe. By Zeus, we meet some strange companions on the road of Hellenism! Thus seemingly abstract philosophies or metaphysical speculations can lead man to deadly conclusions. Political sciences which derive their principles from the sovereignty of man can lead directly to slavery under dictatorships. Political sciences which derive their principles under the laws of nature's God can lead to freedom under democracy. Beware of innocent abstractions.

Can Communism which is so deeply rooted in Atheism ever submit to these concepts? Atheism is also a belief which can be conquered by the still small voice of knowledge. One can not hope to subdue a belief by propaganda or force, especially when such a belief posesses immense forces of atomic weapons. The knowledge of biology conquered Stalin's belief in the Lysensko theory without mortal combat. The self-evident facts of the superiority of free enterprise and rewards of labor through incentives is slowly subduing the basic beliefs of Marxism.

Communists will never submit to the sovereignty of foreign nations without war. This fear of foreign domination inhibits them from freeing themselves from the yoke of dictators. They remember only too well that foreign armies invaded their homes while they were busy throwing off the yoke of Czarism. They equate this predatory struggle for sovereignty with the theory of "The survival of the fittest."

When they will become convinced through demonstrable facts that man has undergone a metamorphosis from animal life to spiritual life, when they will become convinced by self evident facts that man has abandoned his fantasy of dominating all life on earth and the universe, only then might they join humanity and submit to natural moral laws derived from the first law of the universe. They are human and yearn for peace, freedom and survival.

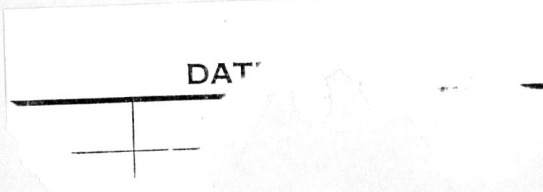